# DOC U MENT
/däkyəmənt/

First meant "instruction" or "evidence," whether written or not.

> *noun* - a piece of written, printed, or electronic matter that provides information or evidence or that serves as an official record
> *verb* - record (something) in written, photographic, or other form
> *synonyms* - paper - deed - record - writing - act - instrument
>
> [Middle English, precept, from Old French, from Latin *documentum*, example, proof, from *docre*, to teach; see dek- in Indo-European roots.]

### Who is responsible for the manufacture of value?

Based on what supercilious ontology have we landed in a space where we vie against other creative people in vain pursuit of the fleeting credibilities of the scarcity economy, rather than freely collaborating and sharing openly with each other in ecstatic celebration of MAKING?

While we understand and acknowledge the economic pressures and fear-mongering that threatens to dominate and crush the creative impulse, we also believe that *now more than ever we have the tools to relinquish agency via cooperative means,* fueled by the fires of the Open Source Movement.

Looking out across the invisible vistas of that rhizomatic parallel country we can begin to see our community beyond constraints, in the place where intention meets resilient, proactive, collaborative organization.

Here is a document born of that belief, sown purely of imagination and will. When we document we assert. We print to make real, to reify our being there. When we do so with mindful intention to address our process, to open our work to others, to create beauty in words in space, to respect and acknowledge the strength of the page we now hold physical, a thing in our hand, we remind ourselves that, like Dorothy: *we had the power all along, my dears.*


### THE PRINT! DOCUMENT SERIES
*is a project of*
the trouble with bartleby
*in collaboration with*
the operating system

# 2018

An Absence So Great and Spontaneous It Is Evidence of Light - Anne Gorrick
The Book of Everyday Instruction - Chloë Bass
Executive Orders Vol. II - a collaboration with the Organism for Poetic Research
One More Revolution - Andrea Mazzariello
Chlorosis - Michael Flatt and Derrick Mund
Sussuros a Mi Padre - Erick Sáenz
Abandoners - Lesley Ann Wheeler
Jazzercise is a Language - Gabriel Ojeda-Sague
Born Again - Ivy Johnson
Attendance - Rocío Carlos and Rachel McLeod Kaminer
Singing for Nothing - Wally Swist
Walking Away From Explosions in Slow Motion - Gregory Crosby
Field Guide to Autobiography - Melissa Eleftherion


KIN(D)* TEXTS AND PROJECTS

Sharing Plastic - Blake Nemec
The Ways of the Monster - Jay Besemer


GLOSSARIUM: UNSILENCED TEXTS AND TRANSLATIONS

The Book of Sounds - Mehdi Navid (Farsi dual language, trans. Tina Rahimi
Kawsay: The Flame of the Jungle - María Vázquez Valdez
(Mexico, trans. Margaret Randall)
Return Trip / Viaje Al Regreso - Israel Dominguez;
(Cuba, trans. Margaret Randall)


*for our full catalog please visit:*
https://squareup.com/store/the-operating-system/

*deeply discounted Book of the Month and Chapbook Series subscriptions
are a great way to support the OS's projects and publications!*
sign up at: http://www.theoperatingsystem.org/subscribe-join/

# 2019

Ark Hive-Marthe Reed
I Made for You a New Machine and All it Does is Hope - Richard Lucyshyn
Illusory Borders-Heidi Reszies
A Year of Misreading the Wildcats - Orchid Tierney
Of Color: Poets' Ways of Making | An Anthology of Essays on Transformative Poetics - Amanda Galvan Huynh & Luisa A. Igloria, Editors

## KIN(D)* TEXTS AND PROJECTS

A Bony Framework for the Tangible Universe-D. Allen
Opera on TV-James Brunton
Hall of Waters-Berry Grass
Transitional Object-Adrian Silbernagel

## GLOSSARIUM: UNSILENCED TEXTS AND TRANSLATIONS

Śnienie / Dreaming - Marta Zelwan/Krystyna Sakowicz, (Poland, trans. Victoria Miluch)
High Tide Of The Eyes - Bijan Elahi (Farsi-English/dual-language) trans. Rebecca Ruth Gould and Kayvan Tahmasebian
In the Drying Shed of Souls: Poetry from Cuba's Generation Zero Katherine Hedeen and Víctor Rodríguez Núñez, translators/editors
Street Gloss - Brent Armendinger with translations of Alejandro Méndez, Mercedes Roffé, Fabián Casas, Diana Bellessi, and Néstor Perlongher (Argentina)
Operation on a Malignant Body - Sergio Loo (Mexico, trans. Will Stockton)
Are There Copper Pipes in Heaven - Katrin Ottarsdóttir (Faroe Islands, trans. Matthew Landrum)

# RECENT & FORTHCOMING OF PRINT::DOCUMENTS and PROJECTS, 2019-20

## 2020

Institution is a Verb: A Panoply Performance Lab Compilation
Poetry Machines: Letters for a Near Future - Margaret Rhee
My Phone Lies to me: Fake News Poetry Workshops as Radical Digital Media Literacy - Alexandra Juhasz, Ed.
Goodbye Wolf-Nik DeDominic
Spite - Danielle Pafunda
Acid Western - Robert Balun
Cupping - Joseph Han


### KIN(D)* TEXTS AND PROJECTS

Hoax - Joey De Jesus
#Survivor - Joanna C. Valente
Intergalactic Travels: Poems from a Fugutive Alien - Alan Pelaez Lopez
RoseSunWater - Angel Dominguez


### GLOSSARIUM: UNSILENCED TEXTS AND TRANSLATIONS

Zugunruhe - Kelly Martinez Grandal (tr. Margaret Randall)
En el entre / In the between: Selected Antena Writings - Antena Aire (Jen Hofer & John Pluecker)
Black and Blue Partition ('Mistry) - Monchoachi (tr. Patricia Hartland)
Si la musique doit mourir (If music were to die) - Tahar Bekri (tr. Amira Rammah)
Farvernes Metafysik: Kosmisk Farvelære (The Metaphysics of Color: A Cosmic Theory of Color) - Ole Jensen Nyrén (tr. Careen Shannon)
Híkurí (Peyote) - José Vincente Anaya (tr. Joshua Pollock)

# WHY PRINT / DOCUMENT?

*The Operating System uses the language "print document" to differentiate from the book-object as part of our mission to distinguish the act of documentation-in-book-FORM from the act of publishing as a backwards-facing replication of the book's agentive \*role\* as it may have appeared the last several centuries of its history. Ultimately, I approach the book as TECHNOLOGY: one of a variety of printed documents (in this case, bound) that humans have invented and in turn used to archive and disseminate ideas, beliefs, stories, and other evidence of production.*

*Ownership and use of printing presses and access to (or restriction of printed materials) has long been a site of struggle, related in many ways to revolutionary activity and the fight for civil rights and free speech all over the world. While (in many countries) the contemporary quotidian landscape has indeed drastically shifted in its access to platforms for sharing information and in the widespread ability to "publish" digitally, even with extremely limited resources, the importance of publication on physical media has not diminished. In fact, this may be the most critical time in recent history for activist groups, artists, and others to insist upon learning, establishing, and encouraging personal and community documentation practices. Hear me out.*

*With The OS's print endeavors I wanted to open up a conversation about this: the ultimately radical, transgressive act of creating PRINT /DOCUMENTATION in the digital age. It's a question of the archive, and of history: who gets to tell the story, and what evidence of our life, our behaviors, our experiences are we leaving behind? We can know little to nothing about the future into which we're leaving an unprecedentedly digital document trail — but we can be assured that publications, government agencies, museums, schools, and other institutional powers that be will continue to leave BOTH a digital and print version of their production for the official record. Will we?*

*As a (rogue) anthropologist and long time academic, I can easily pull up many accounts about how lives, behaviors, experiences — how THE STORY of a time or place — was pieced together using the deep study of correspondence, notebooks, and other physical documents which are no longer the norm in many lives and practices. As we move our creative behaviors towards digital note taking, and even audio and video, what can we predict about future technology that is in any way assuring that our stories will be accurately told – or told at all? How will we leave these things for the record?*

*In these documents we say:*
*WE WERE HERE, WE EXISTED, WE HAVE A DIFFERENT STORY*

*- Elæ [Lynne DeSilva-Johnson], Founder/Creative Director*
*THE OPERATING SYSTEM, Brooklyn NY 2018*

# GLOSSARIUM: UNSILENCED TEXTS

The Operating System's GLOSSARIUM: UNSILENCED TEXTS series was established in early 2016 in an effort to recover silenced voices outside and beyond the canon, seeking out and publishing both contemporary translations and little or un-known out of print texts, in particular those under siege by restrictive regimes and silencing practices in their home (or adoptive) countries. We are committed to producing dual-language versions whenever possible.

Few, even avid readers, are aware of the startling statistic reporting that less than three percent of all books published in the United States, per UNESCO, are works in translation. Less than one percent of these (closer to 0.7%) are works of poetry and fiction. You can imagine that even less of these are experimental or radical works, in particular those from countries in conflict with the US or where funding is hard to come by.

Other countries are far, far ahead of us in reading and promoting international literature, a trend we should be both aware of and concerned about—how does it come to pass that our attentions become so myopic, and as a result, so under-informed? We see the publication of translations, especially in volume, to be a vital and necessary act for all publishers to require of themselves in the service of a more humane, globally aware, world. By publishing 7 titles in 2019, we stand to raise the number of translated books of literature published in the US this year *by a full percent*. We plan to continue this growth as much as possible.

The dual-language titles either in active circulation or forthcoming in this series include Arabic-English, Farsi-English, Polish-English, French-English, Faroese-English, Yaqui Indigenous American translations, and Spanish-English translations from Cuba, Argentina, Mexico, Uruguay, Bolivia, and Puerto Rico.

The term 'Glossarium' derives from latin/greek and is defined as 'a collection of glosses or explanations of words, especially of words not in general use, as those of a dialect, locality or an art or science, or of particular words used by an old or a foreign author.' The series is curated by OS Founder and Managing Editor Elæ [Lynne DeSilva-Johnson,] with the help of global collaborators and friends.

# ABOUT THE TRANSLATORS

## KAYVAN TAHMASEBIAN

is a poet, translator, literary critic, and the author of *Isfahan's Mold* (Sadeqia dar Bayat Esfahan, 2016). His poetry has appeared in *Notre Dame Review*, the *Hawai'i Review*, *Salt Hill*, and *Lunch Ticket*, where it was a finalist for The Gabo Prize for Literature in Translation & Multilingual Texts in 2017. He is co-editor of *The Routledge Handbook of Translation and Activism*.

## REBECCA RUTH GOULD

is the author of the award-winning monograph *Writers & Rebels* (Yale University Press, 2016) and the poetry collection *Cityscapes* (Alien Buddha Press, 2019). She has translated many books from Persian and Georgian, including *After Tomorrow the Days Disappear: Ghazals and Other Poems of Hasan Sijzi of Delhi*(Northwestern University Press, 2016) and *The Death of Bagrat Zakharych and other Stories by Vazha-Pshavela* (Paper & Ink, 2019). She is currently director of the ERC-funded project, "Global Literary Theory"; and Professor, Islamic World & Comparative Literature, at the University of Birmingham.

## ABOUT THE AUTHOR

**BIJAN ELAHI**

was born in 1945. A Persian Modernist poet, Elahi was a leading figure in the she'r-e digar movement, also known as Other Poetry, and did not publish his poems in volumes during his lifetime. After his death in 2010, his work was posthumously published in two volumes: *Didan (Vision)* (Bidgol Publications, 2014) and *Javaniha (Youths)* (Bidgol Publications, 2015).

Rebecca: I first began as a translator from Russian, and then shifted to Georgian and Persian. The experience of memorizing poetry has shaped my practice as a translator of poetry, and served as a visceral reminder to attend to the sound of the poem.

*What does this particular work represent to you both as indicative of your method/creative practice? as indicative of your history? as indicative of your mission/intentions/hopes/plans?*

Kayvan: My method of writing poetry is diametrically opposed to Elahi. My way of writing is less erudite. Translating Elahi has taught me a great about English poetry, and also gave me the opportunity to read Elahi from a foreign point of view, and to discover many creative potentialities that I had not noticed before in the original.

*What would be the best possible outcome for this book? What might it do in the world, and how might its presence as an object facilitate your creative role in your community and beyond? What are your hopes for this book, and for your practice?*

It would be hard to overestimate Elahi's importance as a translator of world poetry into Persian. We hope that readers will recognize in Elahi's poetry the convergence of many styles gathered together from many parts of the world. It has been a great pleasure—and challenge—to first encounter this multifaceted style in Persian and then to render it into English, thereby continuing Elahi's translational process.

# A conversation on translating Elahi with Kayvan Tahmasebian and Rebecca Ruth Gould

*Greetings! Thank you for talking to us about your process today! Can you introduce yourselves, in a way that you would choose? Why do you work in translation?*

*In addition or instead of "translator," what other titles or affiliations do you prefer/feel are more accurate?*

Given that our translations have also inspired to produce scholarship together, we have also come to consider ourselves trancreators. An essay about our creative process and its relationship to translation called "Inspired and Multiple: Poetry, Co-Translation, Creation" appeared in 2019 in the Australian literary journal *Overland*.

*What other work are you doing in the world these days?*

We are now working on a book-length translation of the poetry of Hasan Alizadeh, tentatively entitled *House Arrest*. Some of these poems appeared in *West Branch*, *Tentacular*, *Cordite*, and *Waxwing*.

*Talk about the process or instinct to move this project into book form. How and why did this happen? Have you had this intention for a while?*

We first discussed the project at a bookstore in Isfahan, the city where we met for the first time. The translation of Elahi posed a challenge for us both. We discussed the project for a year, and then produced our first drafts. We then exchanged these drafts after we returned to our respective countries. For the next stages, we traded many drafts using track changes, and then discussed our final versions in person.

*What practices or structures (if any) do you use in the creation of your work, beyond this project?*

Kayvan: Translating French poetry has taught me a lot about translation in general, in particular Mallarmé, Saint-John Perse, Francis Ponge, and Beckett's late prose.

# Acknowledgements

Our work translating Elahi was completed with the support of European Union's Horizon 2020 Research and Innovation Programme under ERC-2017-STG [grant agreement number 759346], within the framework of the "Global Literary Theory" project directed by Rebecca Ruth Gould.

We would like to thank Salmi Elahi, Dariush Kiaras, and Bidgol Publications for permission to publish these poems.

We would also like to thank the following journals, where some of these translations first appeared:

"On Translation," *Wasafiri Magazine* 34(3): 64-68.
"Five Scenes from Icarus," *The Kenyon Review* (2019).
"My Scent that Doesn't Pass," "Dupin Detects," and "Song of the Moon Hanging over the Fields of Damascus," *Two Lines* (2019).
"Birthplace," and "I Laugh for You," *Asymptote* (2019)
"Mourning the Birth of Image," and "Wild Grass," *SAND* 19: 22-27 (2019).
"I Believed," and "Tasseography," *Columbia Journal Online* (2019).
"Eagle," *Poetry Wales* 53.4 (2018): 66-71.
"Dissecting an Onion," *The McNeese Review* 55 (2018): 6-7.
"Douleur d'Après Doyle," *Acumen Literary Journal* 84 (2018): 57-58.
"For two weeks I have been in this palace," *Tin House* (Open Bar) (2017).
"Stations," *Waxwing* XII (2017).

In many cases, the translations have been further edited after their first serial appearance.

Finally, Rebecca would like to thank Beth Gould, Kate Gould, and Brenda Gould for their love and support.

Kayvan would like to thank Mohammad-Baqer Hajiani for his unique support of these translations with his deep archival knowledge of Bijan Elahi's work.

Readers interested in learning more about Elahi may be interested in consulting our website: bijanelahi.hcommons.org. In Persian, news related to Elahi's literary legacy is regularly reported on the Instagram page dedicated to his work (@bijanelahie) and on the Telegram channel: bijan_elahi.

Constantine Cavafy. *Sobh-i ravan* [Departing Morning]. Tehran: Bidgol Publications, 2017. (Including translations of fifty-one poems by Cavafy).

Cyrus Atabay. "Az shab be shab [Night to night]," in *Nazdik-i nur: she'r va zendegi-ye Cyrus Atabay*. Tehran: Peikareh, 2013, 10-66.

Collections of previously published translations

Bijan Elahi (ed.), *Bahaneha-ye ma'nus* [Familiar Pretexts]. Tehran, Bidgol Publications, 2014.

Bijan Elahi (ed.), *Darre-ye alaf-e hezar-rang* [Valley of the Many-Colored Grass]. Tehran: Bidgol Publications, 2016.

Bijan Elahi (ed.), *Zomorod va hamleh: Eliot va Rostand dar kar-i Bijan Elahi* [Emerald and Seizure]. Tehran: Bidgol Publications, 2018. (Including translation of T.S. Eliot's Ash Wednesday (*Charshanba khakestar*), fragments of The Waste Land (*Arz-i mavvat*) and Edmond Rostand's Cyrano de Bergerac (*Lama'at-i namayesh-i Edmon Rostan*).

Scholarship about Elahi's Poetry and Translations

Rebecca Ruth Gould and Kayvan Tahmasebian, "Translation as Alienation: Sufi Hermeneutics and Literary Modernism in Bijan Elahi's Translations," *Modernism/Modernity*

(available at https://hcommons.org/deposits/item/hc:25313/ ).

# Bibliography of Elahi's Work and Translation

### Editions of Elahi's Poems in Persian

*Didan* (Vision). Tehran: Bidgol Publications, 2014.

*Javaniha* (Youths). Tehran: Bidgol Publications, 2015.

### Translations by Elahi

Federico Garcia Lorca, *Gozida-ye ash'ar-e Federico Garcia Lorca* [Selected poetry of Federico Garcia Lorca]. Tehran: Amir Kabir, 1968. Republished in 2003.

T. S. Eliot, *Chahar-shanba khakestar* [Ash Wednesday]. Tehran: Markaz-i nashr-i sepehr, 1972.

Pablo Neruda, *Bist she'r-e 'asheqana va yek sorud-e nowmidi* [Twenty Love Poems and a Song of Despair] (under the pseudonym Forud Khosravani). Tehran: Amir Kabir, 1973.

Mansur-e Hallaj, *Ash'ar-e Hallaj* [Hallaj's Poems]. Tehran: Entesharat-e anjoman-i shahanshahi-ye falsafeh-ye iran, 1975.

Henri Michaux, *Sahat-e javvani* [The Space Within]. Tehran, 1980. Republished as Mostaghallat. Tehran: Bidgol Publications, 2016.

Arthur Rimbaud, *Eshraqha: owraq-e mosavvar* [Illuminations]. Tehran: Faryab, 1983. Republished by Bidgol Publications, 2016.

Mansur-e Ḥallaj, *Ḥallaj al-asrar* [The Works of Hallaj]. Tehran: Bidgol Publications, 2014.

Friedrich Hölderlin, *Niyyat-e khayr* [Good Faith]. Tehran: Bidgol Publications, 2015.

88

transgressions in a poem in the name of poetic license]. Meanwhile I came to realize that, in sublime prose and verse, [such rule-breaking occurs] according to a 'natural exigency', that is, according to what the structure requires, and not because of rhyme limitations. I had already read in Eliot that cultures rely on each other to enrich themselves and they must do so. And now I read in Bahar,[33] the poet laureate, that Bayhaqi had done this under Arabic influence. I saw Bahar is right in this regard but not when he deems it inadmissible.[34] May he rest in peace! Similarly, Gide wrote that the fear of influence comes from the fear of a lack of personality. It is written in the Gospel that the person who attempts to save their self will be deprived of it while the person who sacrifices their self will save it, that is, they will be given eternal life. Then, great men have not feared influence ...

I felt that Bayhaqi, like Nima, had drawn from the street and the book and had mixed them in order to tame them. In other words, he had coupled a wild wolf with a domestic dog to reproduce a third species, namely 'wolfdog', the strong guard. Later when I read *Dārāb-nāma* by Tarsūsi[35] and other folk tales from old days, I confirmed that most of Abu'l Fazl [Bayhaqi]'s words that appear archaic today were drawn from the street rather than from books although his use of everyday language hardly seeks to please the common people by facilitating their understanding. The most certain evidence for this is that [many manuscripts of] his magnum opus has been lost over time. [Bayhaqi] was unable to adapt to the language of his day. Writing was for him fundamentally a craft [*sanāʿat*], both in the sense of art and of alchemy, which is also a branch of philosophy. In this sense, Bayhaqi's history is philosophical prose.

---

33. Muhammad Taqi Bahar, also known as Malik al-Shuara Bahar (1886-1951) was an Iranian poet, literary critic, journalist and politician. His work *Sabk-shināsī* (Stylistics) is the most important history of the evolution of Persian prose to this day.
34. Muhammad Taqi Bahar, *Sabk-shināsī* (Tehran: Amir Kabir, 1958) vol. 2, 70-73.
35. *Dārāb-nāma* (The Book of Darab), a 12th century Persian prose romance written by Abū Tāhir Muhammad ibn Mūsā Tartūsī, recounting the story of legendary King Dārāb. The prose is close to the spoken language of its time.

his poems that I have not found in anyone else. Later, I saw sparks (*sharārahā*) of those things in his letters; What dignified letters, well done! Then I told myself and now I tell you that in modern Iran no great (*kabīr*) figure has emerged in the cultural field except Nima. In those days, I loved him so much that I saw him in my dream one night. He took me to a café and treated me to tea. But he was upset. May he rest in peace.

In those days, we were derided by many. They turned against us, complaining that a child has to learn first and then begin such and such. Fereidun Rahnema[29] gave shelter to the child. May he rest in peace. He said that they were wrong, that Éluard[30] had said that love is the path to knowledge. Later, I encountered Eliot's Dante. I cried when I read in its preface that he had been in love with French poetry long before he was able to translate two lines accurately. I noticed that Nima often chose rough and foul (*khashin va saqat*) words in order to tame them. When I encountered Schoenberg's non-consecutive intervals (*favāsel-i nāmatbū'*), the two ideas sparked the thought in me that I could do something new with the language of official letters, with the language of newspapers, pulp magazines and whatever seemed clichéd. With Ponge,[31] I realized later that I had accidentally become interested in something like the so-called 'anti-poetry'.

Then I was drawn to street talk too ... I encountered Bayhaqi[32] and he fascinated me. Teachers had taught us that the subject comes first, then comes the object and finally the verb that always stands in the end of the sentence according to correct syntax. However, I observed that Bayhaqi does not always follow this rule. He is not a poet to be pardoned by 'poetic exigency', as some ignorant people [say to justify

---

29. Fereidun Rahnema (1930–1975) was an Iranian poet who mentored many key figures in the poetic movement called Other Poetry (shi'r-i dīgar), including Elahi.
30. Paul Éluard (1895–1952) was a French surrealist poet who was influential on modernist Persian poets such as Bijan Elahi and Ahmad Shamlu.
31. Francis Ponge (1899-1988) was a French poet famous for his prose poems on everyday objects, which are devoid of emotions and symbolism.
32. Abu'l Fazl Bayhaqi (995-1077), author of the *Tārīkh-i Bayhaqī* (History of Bayhaqi), the most important source on Ghaznavids. The major part of this voluminous work is lost. It is notable for its prose narrative style.

Now I tend to call it a 'transforming work' (*'amal-i mutahavvil*). For those who have read it, the American writer's prose is ordinary. Someone has described it as 'ordinarily pedantic'. Without quibbling over the example, he can be compared to Bahram Sadeqi[27] whose work cannot be evaluated adequately in terms of its formal technique (*sanā'at-i sūrī*). In other words, Wilder's is an impersonal artificial language (*guftār-i sanī'i naw'i*) as in Tolstoy, as in Kafka, both of whom write in an impersonal artificial language, each in his own way. Unlike Joyce, Beckett, Nabokov, Flaubert, Faulkner, Durrell, Woolf, Stein, James, Musil and Queneau, all of whom write in a personally artificial language (*guftār-i sanī'i shakhsi*). Let's not forget that writers such as Dashiell Hammett and Hemingway try hard to appear ordinary in one way or another. That is, they work according to effaced mannerism (*nahv-i mahv*) while Joyce and Flaubert, for example, chose deliberate mannerism (*sahv-i nahv*), that is, they try to lay bare the traces of their device (*shigird*) and artfulness (*fann*) in the work. Like Rembrandt, who deliberately revealed the turns and strokes of the brush on canvas, and in contrast to Ingres, who effaces in order to appear natural. In Wilder's work, there is nothing of effaced mannerism, let alone deliberate mannerism. He should be evaluated according to totally different criteria. Nonetheless, B who rendered the author's artificial language in his own distinctively artificial style, had worked out an effaced mannerism in my view and I liked it very much. However, the translation did not please C, who asked: 'What about Wilder himself'? B became disappointed and abandoned the work. Finished …

… I was around 14 when I came across a poem by a man named Nima Yushij[28] in a newspaper. Although I did not understand the meaning of "breaking the dream in my wet eyes" (*khāb dar chashm-i taram mīshikanad*), I loved it. The more I read, the more I was drawn to it. It was later that I understood Nima. I learned many things from

---

27. Bahram Sadeqi (1937-1985) was an Iranian short story writer. His only collection of short stories, *Trench and Empty Canteens (Sangar va qumqumehā-yi khālī)* are considered forerunners of modernist experimental fiction depicting the disappointed Iranian society after the 1953 Coup.
28. Nima Yushij (1897-1960) was an Iranian poet who is considered the founder of modernist Persian poetry.

You can see what she looks like although literary norms (*sharāye'-i adabi*) do not permit you to approach her because she is one of your intimates (*mahārim*). However, in Pound's *Classic of Poetry*, the woman is neither forbidden nor your intimate as she has been married to you. You can be near her, she can give birth to your child—creation (*khalq*). Obviously, Pound could not facilitate the marriage of the second one [Waley's version], having known it since 1937, with his culture, since Waley's version was already an intimate to his culture. So, as there was nothing against it, he made the first one he came to know later an intimate to his culture and as I call it, pendant to culture [*āvizeh-yi farhang*], like a yet-unheard-of word that has been inscribed on memory. If he drew upon Waley, it would be called adaptation (*iqtibās*) which was not far from incest (*zenā-yi bā mahārim*). The first [book], however, is waiting to enter into marriage through lawful means. It is unfair if it does not happen, not if it happens. Those who do not permit it: if it is not due to cowardice, it is due to ignorance of literary norms. Such readers have not opened the book of 'poetics [*būtiqā*]' of translation, let alone read it! ...

... I remember–those were the days–when one of our friends–named A–made an accurate draft translation of such and such a novel by the esteemed American story writer Thornton Wilder.[26] It should have been edited and published. Unfortunately, this did not happen. It remained unedited until one of our friends–named B–who loved the novel finally decided to translate it. Then one of our friends–named C–reported to B that A had translated it years before and now D–namely, myself–had it. B was a writer and editor and C was a critic among other things. B was fond of C and kind to me. I was merely a transmitter of the translation. Finally, C suggested that B edit A's drafts instead of retranslating the original. The drafts were linguistically accurate. When the first chapter was complete, C and I went to B's place in the absence of A, who was in exile.

It was not an edited version of the Persian translation (*guzārish*). Rather, it was a retranslation from the original American English.

---

26. Thornton Wilder (1897–1975) was a renowned American playwright and novelist, whose work won the two major American literary prizes: the Pulitzer (three times) and the National Book Award.

exposed briefly here because they belong to the category of confidant translation (*ham-rāzī*). Pound's *Classic of Poetry* appears in 1954.²³ Naturally, it is based on Karlgren's work without needing to reference it. It is from Chinese that he 'translates', not from English! Waley's *Classic of Poetry* appeared in poetic language before these two in 1937.²⁴ However, in a second edition with minor revisions published after Karlgren's work, he deemed it necessary to acknowledge that, in that edition, he had compared the whole work to Karlgren's though he admitted that in some occasions he could not agree with Karlgren in part or in whole.

What if this happened in our part of the world? What would we say, to be fair? We would call Waley the great scholar, may God increase his prodigious knowledge! We would call Waley the faithful translator. If by chance we liked his work, we would call him a talented translator—this is worse than the worst curses. But when it came to Pound, if we considered him 'great', then we would either initiate a silent strike or call him a traitor. If we did not regard him as 'great', then we would comment indifferently that someone had tried to translate and this man had come to 'revise its prose'. We would call it 'rewriting [nigārish]' or 'adaptation [iqtibās]'. Or, we would call it 'translation and rewriting [tarjuma va nigārish]' or 'translation and adaptation [tarjuma va iqtibās]'. While the two last terms are nonsense, the first two are imprecise.

In a sermon, you can use proverbs (*mithāl*) and tell stories, you can give advice and warn. Not so in a scholarly work. The comparability of '*al-shi'r* [poetry]' and '*al-shams* [the sun]'²⁵ does permit a comparison. In Karlgren's Classic of Poetry, the woman is not your intimate (*mahram*). She talks to you through the veil (*pardeh*) since you are forbidden to observe her beauty. In Waley's Classic of Poetry, the woman is not forbidden (*nā-mahram*).

---

23. Ezra Pound, *The Confucian Odes: The Classic Anthology Defined by Confucius* (Cambridge, Mass.: Harvard University Press, 1954).
24. Arthur Waley, *The Book of Songs* (London: Allen & Unwin, 1937).
25. Elahi uses here the Arabic rather than Persian forms for 'poetry' and 'sun' (both are feminine nouns in Arabic).

(*ta'sīrha*), within the canon of English poetry seems unquestionable today. However, Pound is not only a poet but also the grand master of poetics and one of the greatest pioneers of modern culture.

His translations do not originate from a translational (*dīlmāj*) principle; they not only give lessons in poetry but also add an entry to the universal glossary of 'knowledge [*'ilm*]' in its broadest sense. It has been claimed that after Pound, translating and rereading the ancient poets is like observing art after Picasso! When it comes to Karlgren, we are no longer talking about poetry and the poet —we are faced with a great Sinologist, someone analogous to Norberg and Henning vis-à-vis our culture.[20]

Karlgren's work on *Classic of Poetry* first appears successively from 1942 to 1946 in *Bulletin of the Museum of Far Eastern Antiquities* in Stockholm, Sweden. *The Classic of Poetry* appeared in a volume in Stockholm in 1950.[21] In September 1975, I accidentally picked up the volume in London.[22] It made me extremely happy because I had read Pound's *Classic of Poetry* in 1971 and I knew that it was based on Karlgren's work. I had seen some of his other works before. Each poem in Karlgren's *Classic of Poetry* is presented in four sections. First, the original Chinese, then its transliteration into Roman letters with a presentation of the rhyme schemes, then a word by word translation into English prose and finally notes (where needed) on lexicon, syntax and so on. Altogether this amounts to a 'dream' for a lover, a poet-translator, for Pound who understood as much Chinese as you and I do except that he is vastly different from you and I. Firstly, Pound is a genius and we are not. Secondly, he has read extensively in Sinology. Thirdly, given his polyglotism and profound poetic talent, it was possible to reach, through philological veils, the seed (*nutfa*) at the heart (*batn*) of the foreign poet. Nevertheless, Pound's purposes lie basically beyond these words and I am afraid they cannot be

---

20. Matthias Norberg, (1747–1826) was a Swedish professor of Greek and Oriental languages at Lund University. Walter Bruno Henning (1908-1967) was a German scholar of Middle Iranian languages and literature.
21. See Bernhard Karlgren, *The Book of Odes* (Stockholm: Museum of Far Eastern Antiquities, 1950).
22. Elahi resided in London from 1970 to 1972.

imposes, and the latter faithful to the rules the rewriter chooses to the extent that the rewriter's chosen rules entirely or partly correspond to the writer's imposed rules in one way or another.

The second type, namely 'free' translation, is itself divided into two completely different categories. One, as we call it, is confidant (*hamrāzi*) translation that goes beyond intimacy (*damsāzi*) and may suggest a shared secret (*sirr*), form (*lawn*)[19] and structure (*sākht*) respectively corresponding to the hidden meaning (*bātin*), the apparent meaning (*zāhir*), and what brings them together. The purpose of this type of translation is creativity (*khalq*) on different levels and for different purposes.

The second subdivision of free translation, however, tends toward aimless wandering (*āzād-ravī*). Appropriation (*tasarruf*) is another name for this type of translation or rather 'appropriation and alteration [*dakhl va tasarruf*]'. I have denominated these two completely separate categories by two opposite terms, two antithetical correlatives: alteration (*dakhl*) and creation (*khalq*) …

… Let me give an example. *Wu Ching*, or *The Five Classics* of the Confucian canon, is familiar to scholars. It consists of *Shu Ching (Classic of History)*, *Li Chi (Collection of Rituals)*, *Shih Ching (Classic of Poetry)*, *Ch'un Ch'iu (Spring and Autumn Annals)* and finally *I Ching (Classic of Changes)*, the Chinese book of divination. Only three translations of Classic of Poetry are considered here. For weeks, I have learned a lot from frequent comparisons I made between three translations into English by Bernhard Karlgren, Arthur Waley and Ezra Pound.

More than scholarly research, Waley's work is a translation of Chinese and Japanese principles and often poetry. No one can deny that Waley is a perfect poet for the hundreds of Chinese poems he translated into English. The inclusion of these translations, or 'influences'

---

19. *Lawn* originally means 'color'.

It is imposed by the translator who is often a person of minimal ability, undoubtedly less capable than the original writer. The translator may often be someone unable to write poetry, unable to write fiction, unable to think and investigate, who has only taken refuge (*panāh*) in this field. In this way and in this atmosphere, translation is often the repressed complex of creation. However, we agree with those who consider translation as a re-creation (*bāz-āfarinish*) even more difficult than the original. If creation (*āfarinish*) is viewed as a dance, translation is a dance in chains [*raqs dar zanjīr*]. When translating Shakespeare, you should fly as high as him though with tied wings. Translation, like authorship, can be accomplished in different ways and fashions. This is only one of those ways which serves meanwhile as a foundation for all others. Opposed to the above notion, I attempted in several books to prove the dictum 'the more accurate, the more beautiful' as long as our perception of beauty is purified from the static. Accuracy, it can be argued, is guaranteed by dictionaries as well. Those books are Rimbaud's prose poems, Flaubert's tale[18] and this Hölderlin. Although all three enter late into Persian, as expected they bring to our language unknown or lesser known beauty and fresh taste, just as they introduced into their own language less known beauty or unknown beauty. The latter better describes Hölderlin's language and mood ...

### III.   From Elahi, *Translation in Every Words* (1985)

... The question is the 'polarity' of the world of translation. This time, take one side as the writer (generally speaking, the poet, story writer, philosopher, mystic and so on), the other side as the rewriter where the term signifies the translator. Then say that translation generally consists of two types, bound (*muqayyad*) and free (*mukhtār*). The former is done according to imposed rules, the latter according to chosen rules. If appropriately done, both types of translation are faithful, except that the former is faithful to the rules the writer

---

18. Elahi's translation of Gustave Flaubert's tale, *La légende de Saint-Julien l'hospitalier (The Legend of Saint Julian the Hospitalier)* published in *Bahānahā-yi ma'nūs (Familiar Excuses)* (Tehran: Bidgol Publications, 2014).

On occasions when the teller cannot keep both levels in balance as their language and culture requires, that is, when the teller is obliged to transition from apparent to hidden and vice versa, they should critically decide which level of the text, i.e. the essence of the text, has more presence in its new life. Particularly at stake here is poetry and whatever has a poetic presence in the realm of *poiesis* (*ʿālam-i tadvīnī*). Without *presence*, a poem would be undoubtedly deprived of its necessary meaning because 'meaning' is only one of the necessary conditions of such a presence …

Our poets have not paid enough attention to prose poems. My experiments in this field (after two models, two signatures [*raqam*], namely Rimbaud and Michaux) are a challenge or trial anyway. Let's not forget what we read, whether a success or a failure, is a poem in Persian

## II. From *Tadhakkur*, the 1975 note appended to Elahi's translation of Friedrich Hölderlin's selected poems (published as *Niyat-i khayr* (Good Faith), Tehran, 2015)

From a certain point of view, my Hölderlin is the opposite of my Hallaj.[17] In order to elucidate the point of view, one needs to elicit a common, therefore popular, lukewarm and reactionary (*murtajiʿ*) perception of translation typical of an impotent perceiver: 'Translation is either accurate or beautiful; If beautiful then not accurate, if accurate then not beautiful.' With a few exceptions, our literary translators have a static idea of beauty. Like rhinos with stiff necks, they can see only what lies ahead and are deprived of a tuning eye (*nigah-i gardān*). Furthermore, they are not even accurate. Most translations into Persian end up one and a half times the length of the original text. Where the translated text is difficult and at an unreasonable distance from the original, beauty does not truly come from the original and from any truth whatsoever.

---

17. Elahi is referring to his translation of the Sufi Arabic poet Mansur Abu Hallaj, which differs radically in style from his Hölderlin translations. See Bijan Elahi, trans. *Hallāj al-asrār (akhbār va ashʿār)* [*The secret Hallaj: stories and poems*] (Tehran: Bidgol Publications, 2014 [1975]).

# On Translation[15]
# by Bijan Elahi

I. From *Ishāra* (Indication), the preface to Elahi translation of Arthur Rimbaud's *Illuminations* (Ishrāqhā, Tehran, 1984)

... we should distinguish between ... a translator who is called 'performer [*'āmil*]' and the one who can be called 'teller [*nāqil*]'. 'Freedom' of translation is conceptually different with regard to these two terms. Everywhere, everything can be defined in innumerable ways depending on the innumerable possibilities available in each situation. In this brief definition, however, these two are separated not by choice but by what the text at hand requires. A translator as teller can often work as a performer, and vice versa, depending on the text they choose to translate. It is a general problem that we have not distinguished between the two types of translation because we do not distinguish between performative texts and stories. Our perception of translation has unfortunately been restricted to 'telling [*naql*]'. As a result, there are few good translations of performative texts, including much poetry translation.

Without wishing to enter into details, I can briefly state that the teller (*nāqil*) works within the limits of a reporter while the performer (*'āmil*) works within the limits of an executor. The translator's relation to the text is that of a director to the play, of a filmmaker to the script, and of a singer to the song. The song is already composed by someone else to be sung by her. Or as with traditional painters who co-drafted a single canvas: one sketched and the other finished.

A good teller narrates precisely the outer (*zāhir*) level of an event. The translator as performer, however, must precisely act out the event simultaneously on both the outer and inner (*bātin*) levels.

---

15. For the Persian text used here, see Bijan Elahi, "On Translation [*Dar bāb-i tarjumeh*]," in *In Shumāreh bā ta'khīr* [The issue delayed], ed. M. Taher Nokandeh (Tehran: Avanevesht, 2011), volume 6: 46-57.
16 The pair can also be translated as 'outside/inside' and 'appearance/heart'.

[~]

حس می کردم که بیهقی نیز، چنان نیما، از کوچه و از کتاب گرفته و در هم زده تا رام کند. یعنی گرگِ وحشی گرفته و جفت انداخته یا سگِ اهلی تا به نسل سومی برسد: «سگِ گرگی» که پاسبانی‌ست قدر قدرت. بعدها که «داراب نامه»‌ی طرسوسی و داستانهای عامیانه‌ی دیگری خواندم از آن روزگار دور، دیدم آری، خیلی از واژگان بوالفضل - که ادبایی می نماید امروزه - از کوچه بوده، نه از کتاب. ولی چنین نکرده که مردمپسند و عوام فهم بگرداند. شاهد صادق این که شاهکار او رفته رفته از دست می رود، که دشوار بوده که یعنی در خور گنجایش روزگارش نمی بوده و دشوار بوده چون «صناعت» بوده که همزمان به معنی‌ی هنر و به معنی‌ی کیمیاگری‌ست که خود «فلسفه» نیز نامیده شده‌ست و تاریخ بیهقی «نثر فلسفی»‌ست به این معنا.

دیرترها، اما، شراره‌هایی از آن «چیزها» در نامه‌های خودش دیدم: چه نامه‌های متینی، به به! پس آنگاه به خودم گفتم و اینک به تو می‌گویم که در ایران نوین هیچ "کبیر"ی نیامده در هیچ زمینه‌ی فرهنگی الا نیما و من از بس که دوستش داشتم آن ایام، شبی به خوابش دیدم. قهوه‌خانه‌ام برد و چای داد. اما غمگین بود و پکر. خدا بیامرزد.

آن زمان خیلی‌ها به ریش ما خندیدند، لج خیلی‌ها بالا آمد، که طفل اول باید برود سواد یاد بگیرد، بعد فلان و بهمان بکند! فریدون رهنما، ولی، به طفل پناهی داد. خدا بیامرزد. گفت غلط کرده‌اند! الوار گفته مهرورزی راه شناسایی‌ست! دیرترها، به «دانته»ی الیوت برخوردم. در مقدمه‌اش به گریه افتادم. می‌نویسد من دیوانه‌ی شعر فرانسوی بودم، دیری از آن پیش که قادر به ترجمه‌ی صحیح دو مصرع باشم! باری، من نگاه می‌کردم می‌دیدم نیما چه بسا «خشن و سقط» اختیار می‌کند از کلام تا رام کند. پس به «فواصل نامتبوع» شوئنبرگ که برخوردم، هر دو [دریافت] به هم خورد و جرقه زد. کم کمک به فکر افتادم با زبان نامه‌های اداری، با زبان روزنامه‌ها و رنگین نامه‌ها و آنچه باسمه‌یی می‌نمود، کار تازه‌یی بکنم که دیرترها، از راه پونژ دانستم خفته خفته رویکرد به چیزی از قبیل «ضد شعر » داشته‌ام به اصطلاح.

پس به زبان [~] بازار و کوچه هم جلب شدم. به بیهقی برخوردم. گرفت، سخت. اساتید گفته بودند که اول فاعل، بعد مفعول و فعل همیشه در ته جمله‌ست که می‌افتد و این یعنی نحو درست!

می‌دیدم بیهقی بر این نمی‌رود چه بسا. شعر هم نگفته از «ضرورت شعری» باشد به اصطلاح مشتی پرت. چندی که گذشت، دانستم این، چه در نظم و چه در نثر، اگر که والا باشند، از «ضرورت حقیقی» است، یعنی به مقتضای ساختار، نه که از تنگی‌ی قافیه. در الیوت خوانده بودم از آن پیش که فرهنگ‌ها به هم تکیه می‌زنند که اغنای خود کنند و ضروریست چنین کنند! و اینک در ملک الشعرای بهار می‌خواندم که بیهقی تحت «تأثیر» لسان العرب چنین کرده و می‌دیدم که راست گفته و پرت فهمیده که ناپسند دانسته، روانش شاد! ژید هم، اما، نوشته که ترس از «تأثیر» جز ترس از فقدان شخصیت نیست، حال آن که در «انجیل» گفته هر کس به نجات خویش بکوشد محروم می‌شود، ولی هر که خویشتن [فدا] کند نجاتِ خویشتن داده، که یعنی زندگی‌ی راستین بدو ( به «خویشتن») بخشیده. پس بزرگان از تأثیر غیر نترسیده‌اند.

دوستان ما – نامش «ب» – که عاشق داستان شده بود، سرانجام، تصمیم به ترجمه‌اش گرفت و پارسال بود انگار. پس یکی از دوستان ما – نامش «ج» – به «ب» خبر داد که «الف» ترجمه کرده سال‌ها پیش و پیش فلانی‌ست که یعنی بنده، «ب» نویسنده و ویراستار بود و «ج» از جمله، منتقد بود و پس «ب» ارادتی به «ج» داشت و لطفی نیز به من، که این میان «عمله‌ی ترجمه» من بودم و بس. پس بنا شد، به پیشنهاد «ج»، که «ب» جای بازگردانی از اصل، به ویرایش گزارش «الف» بنشیند که، نظر به «زبان» اصل، بس دقیق بود. فصل اول از کار درآمد و من و «ج» به خانه‌ی «ب» رفتیم و «الف» نبود، در غربت بود.

کار ویراسته‌ی گزارش فارسی نبود، بازگردانی بود از اصل آمریکایی، و از همین باب بود که من اکنون «عمل متحول» می‌نامم. نثر آن نویسنده‌ی آمریکایی، اگر بشناسی، عادی‌ست، البته «عادی‌ی آقا معلمی» به قول کسی؛ و، بی مناقشه در مثل، گیر چیزی از قبیله‌ی بهرام صادقی که صناعت صوری را نقشی اساسی نیست در ارزمندی‌ی کار او. یعنی «گفتار صنیعی‌ی نوعی» دارد، مثلاً چون تالستوی، مثلاً چون کافکا، که هر دو «گفتار صنیعی‌ی نوعی» دارند. گرچه هر کدام به نوعی دیگر، و نه چون جویس، چون پروست، چون بکت، چون نابوکف، یا فلوبر، یا فاکنر، یا دارل، یا ویرجینیا وولف، یا گرترود استاین، یا که هنری جیمز و موزیل و کنو، که «گفتار صنیعی‌ی شخصی» دارند. و از یاد مبر چون کسانی چون دشیل همت و همینگ‌وی نیز سخت تراشیده کار می‌کنند که عادی نمایی کنند به نحوی، یعنی به «نحوِ محو» می‌خواهند کار کنند؛ حال آن که، فی‌المثل، در فلوبر، یا جویس، «صحوِ نحو» دیده می‌شود، یعنی می‌کوشند اثر شگرد و داغِ پای «فن» در زمینه‌ی کار عیان باشد، مثلاً چون رامبراند که عامدانه می‌خواهد گردش و زخم قلم در نگاره پیدا باشد، برعکس انگر که محو می‌کند تا «طبیعی» جلوه نماید کار.

کار وایلدر خبر از «نحو محو» هم نمی‌دهد، چه رسد به «صحو محو»، ارزمندی‌ی او بناست به چیز دیگری باشد. با این همه، «ب» – که از «گفتار صنیعی‌ی نوعی»ی نویسنده رفته بود به «گفتار صنیعی‌ی شخصی» – به «نحوِ محو» کار کرده بود از چشم من و سخت پسندیده. «ج» ولی، نپسندید، یعنی «درست» ندانست چنین کردن: وایلدر این میان چه می‌شود؟! «ب» دلسرد شد، کنار گذاشت. پایان کار. تق ! [~]

*

[~] و چیزی حوالی‌ی چارده سالم بود که در روزنامه‌ها برخوردم به شعری از مردی به نام نیما یوشیج: «خواب در چشم ترم می‌شکند...» ندانستم یعنی چه، ولی جذبم کرد و، هر چه بیشتر می‌خواندم، بیشتر جذب می‌شدم. بعدها بود که نیماشناس شدم: چیزها یاد گرفتم از شعر او که هنوز هم ندیده‌ام در سخن کسی.

اگر این اتفاق در این گوشه‌ی دنیا افتاده بود، چه می‌گفتیم؟ انصاف را! چه می‌گفتیم؟ یحتمل به کارلگرن می‌گفتیم فاضل مفضال، دامت افاضاته العالیه! به وی لی می‌گفتیم که مرد امین. اگر از کارش هم دست بر قضا خوشمان می‌آمد، می‌گفتیم مترجم با ذوق، که یعنی از فحش خارمادر بدتر! ولی به پاوند که می‌رسیدیم، اگر به چشم مان «گنده» میامد، یا اعتصاب سکوت می‌کردیم، یا که خائنش می‌خواندیم؛ اگر به چشم مان «گنده» نمی‌آمد، به خونسردی برگزار می‌کردیم که آقا، یکی آمده زحمت کشیده «ترجمه» کرده، این یکی برداشته «نشرش را درست کرده» و می‌گفتیم «نگارش»، می‌گفتیم «اقتباس». یا می‌گفتیم «ترجمه و نگارش»، می‌گفتیم «ترجمه و اقتباس» دو لفظ آخرین، مهمل. دو لفظ اولین، بی «حد».

در وعظ می‌توان مثال زد و قصه گفت، می‌توان پند داد و هشدار داد؛ در تحقیق نمی‌توان! «الشعر» که سنجیدنی ست با «الشمس» (مؤنث)، به ما جواز تشبیه می‌دهد. در «سرودنامه»ی کارلگرن، زن به شما محرم نیست، از پس پرده با شما حرف می‌زند، زیارت جمال او بر شما ممنوع، در «سرودنامه»ی وی لی، زن به شما نامحرم نیست، می‌توانید ببینید چه شکلی‌ست، ولی شرایع ادبی به شما اجازه نمی‌دهد که به او نزدیک شوید، چون که خود از محارم شماست. ولی، در «سرودنامه»ی پاوند، زن نه نامحرم شماست، نه از محارم‌تان، چون به عقد شما درآمده؛ می‌توانید به او نزدیک شوید، می‌تواند برای شما بچه بیاورد («خلق»). پیداست که پاوند دومی را، که از ۱۹۳۷ می‌شناخت، نمی‌توانست به عقد فرهنگ خود در آورد، که از محارم بود! پس اولی را، که بعدها شناخت، چون مانعی نداشت، محرم فرهنگ کرد و «آویزه‌ی فرهنگ»، به اصطلاح این بنده، چون سخنی ~ از آن پیش نانیوشیده ~ که دیگر آویزه‌ی گوش. آری، از وی لی اگر می‌گرفت، «اقتباس» می‌بود، که در این مقام چندان دور از زنای محارم نیست! ولی، اما، خود منتظر نشسته که از راههای قانونی به عقد درآید. پس اگر نکنند، بی انصافی‌ست، نه اگر عقد کنند! حضرات! که مجاز نمی‌دانند، اگر از نامردی نبوده باشد، باری، از بی اطلاعی از شرایع ادبی‌ست، که «بوطیقا»ی ترجمه را باز نکرده‌اند، چه رسد که بخوانند! [~]

*

[~] خاطره یی نقل می‌کنم. همین پارسال بود انگار. روزگاری یکی از دوستان ما ــ نامش «الف» ــ ترجمه یی دقیق کرده بود، به گزارش خام البته، از رمانی نامش چنین و چنان، نوشته‌ی وایلدر، داستان نویس گرانمایه‌ی آمریکایی. بایستی ویراسته می‌شد و چاپ، که نشد از بدِ روزگار و ماند و ماند و ماند تا یکی از

که از منطق «دیلماج» آب نمی خورد، نه همین درس شاعری، که توانسته واژه‌ای به فرهنگ جهانی‌ی «علم» بیفزاید ( به معنای اعّم )، چنان که نوشته‌اند که ترجمه و بازخوانی‌ی شعر قدما، پس از او، چنان هنر نقاشی‌ست پس از پیکاسو! و اما به کار لگرن که می‌رسیم، دیگر سخن از شعر و شاعری به هیچ روی نیست، تنها با چین‌شناسی مواجهیم استاد، مردی از قبیل نوبرگ هنینگ که منتها در زمینه‌ی فرهنگ ماست که کار کرده‌اند.

کار کارلگرن، روی «سرود نامه» جسته جسته چاپ می شود نخست، از ۱۹۴۲ تا ۱۹۴۶، در بیلکهای تحویلخانه‌ی عتیقه‌های خاور دور، استکهلم سوئد. این «سرودنامه» به هیأت کتاب، در ۱۹۵۰ در میاید، باز در استکهلم، بنده هم، در شهریور ۵۴ ( ۱۳۵۴ البته )، از قضا، نسخه‌یی می یابم در لندن و کم مانده بود از ذوق که دیوانه شوم. چه «سرودنامه»ی پاوند را در ۱۳۵۰ خوانده بودم، و دانسته که از روی کارلگرن کار شده‌ست ( پاری از دیگر آثار مرد را پیش از اینها می‌شناخته‌ام.) هر سرود «سرودنامه»، در کار کارلگرن، در چهار بخش شناسانده شده. نخست اصل چینی‌ست. سپس ترانویسی‌ی اصل به حروف رومی ست (latin)، با نمایشی از نظام قافیه‌ها، سپس ترجمه‌یی‌ست، لفظ به لفظ، به نثر انگلیسی. سپس یادداشت‌هایی‌ست (بایسته اگر می نموده) در لغویات و دستوریات و غیرها. یعنی که روی هم "رویا" - رؤیای عاشقی، شاعر/ ترجمان، چنان پاوند که از چینی به همان مایه حالی‌ی او می‌شود که حالی‌ی من و تو! الا، شخصاً، عظیم فرق می کند با من و تو. اولاً نابغه‌ست، که من و تو نیستیم. ثانیاً زیاد خوانده در زمینه‌ی چینیات، ثالثاً چند زبانه‌ست و، این که به شمّ قوی‌ی شاعری علاوه شود، شاید بتوان به "نطفه"ی شعری - از ورای موانع فقه اللنوی - چنگ انداخت در "بطن" شاعری بیگانه. وانگهی مقاصد او، اصلاً، ورای این حرفهاست که می افتد و اینجا (متأسفم) به اشاره نیز بر گزار نتواند شد، چون که از مقوله‌ی «همرازی»ست. پس «سرودنامه» ی پاوند در ۱۹۵۴ در می آید، طبعاً از روی کارلگرن، ولی بی که هیچ نیازی حتا به ذکر مأخذ باشد: از چینی‌ست که او «ترجمه» می کند، نه که از انگلیسی! «سرودنامه»ی وی لی، به زبان شعر، خود پیش از این دو درآمده، در ۱۹۳۷. با این همه، در ویرایش ثانوی که با تصحیحاتی جزئی پس از «سرودنامه»ی کارلگرن چاپخش می‌شود، مرد با خود فریضه می داند که اشاره کند کل کار را - در این ویرایش - با کار کارلگرن سنجیده‌، اگرچه دیده در بسا جاها همداستان او نیست بیش و کم یا به هیچ روی.

اعم: شاعر و داستان نویس و عالم و عارف و که و که)، دومی بازنویسنده، اگر تعبیری از مترجم باشد. پس بگو ترجمه کلاً دو گونه می شود «مقید» و «مختار». اولی با قواعد اعمالی ست، دومی با قواعد اختیاری. هر دو ترجمان هم، اگر که شایسته‌اند، وفادارند؛ الا اولی وفادار قواعدی‌ست که نویسنده اعمال می‌کند، دومی وفادار قواعدی که بازنویسنده اختیار می‌کند، همزمان که قواعد اختیاری‌ی بازنویسنده کلاً یا بعضاً ناظر به قواعد اعمالی‌ی نویسنده‌ست به هر اعتباری از اعتبارها.

«ترجمه‌ی مختار» یعنی که دومی، خود دو مقوله‌ی کاملاً جداست. یعنی، به نامگذاری‌ی ما، «همرازی» ست که خود، گذشته از دمسازی، رسانای اشتراک در سرّ و لون و ساخت تواند بود ( ناظر به باطن و ظاهر و رابطه‌ی آن دو). قصد این ترجمه آفرینندگی است («خلق») در سطوح مختلف به مقاصد مختلف. [~ ]

دومی، اما، قصدش آزادروی است ( مقوله‌ی ثانی از همان «ترجمه‌ی مختار» ). «تصرف» به همین ترجمه گفته‌اند، یا که «دخل و تصرف». از این دو مقوله‌ی کاملاً جدا، در مقام رویارویی (یعنی هرگاه که در قبال هم، یا که بالنسبه‌ی هم، یاد شوند)، بنده به «دخل» و «خلق» عبارت کرده‌ام. [~ ]

٭

[~ ] مثالی بزنم. «خمسه‌ی صینیه»، که «پنجنامه» مکتب کنفسیوس باشد (Wu Ching)، آشنای اهل مطالعه‌ست: «کارنامه» یا «أخبارالأوائل» (Ching Shu)، «آئین نامه» یا «تطریس الشمائر» (Li Chi)، «سرودنامه» یا «مجمع الأنشاد» (Shih Ching)، «گاهنامه» یا «امهات المواقیت» (Chun Chiu)، که همان فالنامه‌ی چینی‌ست. نظر، این میان، به سه ترجمه‌ی «سرودنامه»ست فقط، از مقایسه‌ی چندباره‌ی این سه ترجمه‌ی انگلیسی، در طول هفته‌ها، من چه بسیار که آموخته‌ام! یکی کار کارلگرن (Bernhard Karlgren)، آن یکی کار وی لی (Arthur Waley)، سومی کار پاوند (Ezra Pound).

کار وی لی، گذشته از تحقیق، اساساً ترجمه بوده از اصول چینی و ژاپنی، چه بسا که شعر. ولی احدی نیست که وی لی به چشم او، نظر به همان چند سد شعر چینی‌ی گردانده به انگلیسی، «برای خودش یک پا شاعر» نباشد. جایگیری‌ی این ترجمه‌ها (= تأثیرها) در شعر انگلیسی زبان دیگر انکار ناپذیر می‌نماید امروزه. پاوند، ولی، نه تنها شاعر، که استاد بزرگ شعر و یکی از اعاظم سازندگان فرهنگ معاصر به شمار می‌آید. ترجمه‌های او،

از « تذکر » ( « نیت خیر » هُلدرلین )

هلدرلین من، از نظری، نقطه‌ی مقابل حلاج منست. ذکر این که از چه نظر، اشاره‌یی می‌طلبد به تصوری همه‌گیر، در نتیجه عوامانه، فاتر و مرتجع، درباره‌ی ترجمه – زاده از ناتوانی‌ی متصور: «ترجمه یا دقیق یا زیباست؛ اگر زیباست دقیق نیست؛ و اگر دقیق زیبا نیست.» استثناها به کنار، مترجمان ادبی ما نشان داده‌اند که از زیبایی تصور ایستایی دارند؛ چون کرگدنند، با گردنی که نمی‌گردد، که همین پیش روی را می‌بینند، و عاری از "نگاهی گردان"؛ گذشته از این که دقیق هم نیستند: اکثر ترجمه‌های فارسی، کم و بیش، نیم چندان اضافه بر اصل است از لحاظ حجم. و آن جا که بناست متن زیبا باشد – که یعنی سخت، و بی دلیل، دور از اصل – زیبایی از حقیقتِ اصل نمی‌آید، و از هیچ حقیقتی نمی‌آید، چیزی تحمیلی‌ست، از سوی مترجم، که بسا که آدمی کم مایه‌ست، کم مایه‌تر از شخص نویسنده به حتم؛ بسا که آدمی‌ست واماند‌ه از سرودن شعر، واماند‌ه از نوشتن قصه، و واماند‌ه از اندیشه و جستجو، که به این عرصه "پناه" آورده. ترجمه، این گونه، در این محیط، چه بسا عقده‌ی سرکوفته‌ی آفریند‌گیست. ما، اما، همد‌هان با برخی، آن را بازآفرینشی می‌شمریم، به اعتباری البته، دشوارتر از آفرینش اصلی – به این اعتبار که آفرینش اگر رقصی‌ست، ترجمه رقصی‌ست در زنجیر: در ترجمه‌ی شکسپیر، باید بکوشی همبال شکسپیر بپری اما با پر بسته! بگذریم از این که ترجمه هم، چون تألیف، به شیوه‌ها و راه‌های گون‌گون تواند رفت. این یکی از راه‌هاست، که، در ضمن، جنبه‌ی پایه دارد و شالوده. من، به ستیز با تصور مذکور، در کتابی چند کوششی داشتم به اثبات این که «هر چه دقیق‌تر، زیباتر» اگر، البته، دریافت زیبایی مان گند‌زدایی شود از کثافت و ایستایی، و لطیف. دقت را، می توان حتا گفت، واژه نامه‌ها تضمین می‌کنند. از آن چند کتاب، یکی شعرهای نثری‌ی رمبوست، یکی قصه‌ی فلوبر، یکی هم همین هلدرلین. گرچه هر سه چنین دیر به فارسی می‌آیند، باید انتظار داشت زیبایی‌های ناشناخته یا کم شناخته‌یی به زبان ما بیاورند، طعمی «تازه»: همچنان که در زبان خود نیز زیبایی‌ی کم شناخته‌یی آوردند، یا « ناشناختهٌ»یی – صفتی که با زبان و جوّ هلدرلین سازگار می‌نماید. [~]

از « ترجمه از زبان عالم و آدم » [۱۳۶۳]

[~] سخن از « دو قطبی»ی عالم ترجمه رفت. این باره بگیر اولی نویسنده‌ست ( به معنای

# در باب ترجمه

از « اشاره » ( «اشراقها»ی رمبو )
[ ~ ] باید این جا متوجه فرق مترجمی بود که [ ~ ] « عامل » خوانده ایم با مترجمی که می توان «ناقل» خواند. "آزادی"ی یک ترجمه، مفهوماً، در مورد این و آن تفاوتِ کلی دارد. همه جا، از همه چیز، می توان تعاریف بی شماری به دست داد، نظر به امکانات بیشمار که در هر زمینه هست در تعریف محقر فعلی، اما، این دو، نه از روی اختیار، که به مقتضای متن کار، سوای هم می افتند. مترجم ناقل گاه می تواند عامل باشد - و کذلک بالعکس - بسته به متنی که برای ترجمه بر می دارد. مشکل ما همه، اما، این که دو ترجمان، هنوز، از هم شناخته نیستند، چرا که میان دو متن فرق نگذاشته ایم. تصور ما از ترجمه محدود به «نقل» بوده بدبختانه، لذا هرگز آش دهنسوزی بیرون نداده ایم در ترجمه‌ی شعر فی المثل.
لبّ تعریف ( بی حال و مجال هیچ تفصیلی ) این که ناقل در حدِّ "خبرنگار" کار می کند. عامل در حد "مجری" - رابطه اش با متن رابطه ی کارگردان با نمایشنامه، فیلمساز با فیلمنامه، و آوازخوان با آواز: آوازی که دیگری به نغمه در آورده است، تا او به "صدا" در آورد؛ یا چنان که نقاشان سنتی، گاهی، دو تنه روی یک پرده کار می کردند: یک «رقم» می زد، یکی « عمل » می آورد. [ ~ ]
ناقل خوب عین واقعه را «نقل» می کند در سطح "ظاهر" و "باطن" و گاه اگر، به مقتضای فرهنگ و زبان خود، حفظ تعادل میان هر دو سطح، یعنی اگر گاه ناچار شود و اگراید از "ظاهر" به نفع "باطن" یا بالعکس، باید ناقدانه بسنجد که متن، گوهر متن، در این زایش تازه، در کدام یک از دو سطح بیشتر «حضور» می یابد. این جا، بخصوص، صحبت از شعر می کنیم و هر آنچه حضوری شاعرانه دارد در عالم تدوینی، و می افزاییم: چرا که شعر اگر «حضور» نداشته باشد، معنای لازم شعر را بی گمان نخواهد داشت، که «معنا» خود جز از لوازم این «حضور» نیست.[ ~ ]
تجربه های حقیر در این زمینه ( از روی دو الگو ) دو "رقم": رمبو، و میشو) چالش یا کوششی ست به هر صورت: از یاد نمی بریم آنچه می خوانیم، ضعیف یا قوی، «شعر فارسی» ست.

"even more difficult than the original." Elahi's conceptualisation of creation as a form of possession by an external force reveals the close kindship he perceives between translation and creation. These details are explored more fully in our article, "Translation as Alienation: Sufi Hermeneutics and Literary Modernism in Bijan Elahi's Translations" (see the Bibliography).

Given the gender neutrality of the Persian third-person pronoun, we have generally rendered the singular third-person pronoun by they/them whenever possible, and have only indicated a gender when grammatically unavoidable. Ellipses in the translated text reflect the punctuation of the original; the text has been translated in full.

## Translator's Introduction to Bijan Elahi, "On Translation"

In 2011, the poet and distinguished translator of Italian literature Mohsen Taher Nokandeh gathered together the writings on translation by the great avant-garde Iranian poet Bijan Elahi (1945-2010) under the heading 'On Translation'. These writings are translated here for the first time, in part for the light they shed on Elahi's original poetic creations. The first two selections were published as prefaces to Elahi's translations. The third selection comprises Elahi's notes towards an unpublished monograph on translation, initiated and abandoned in 1985, which he planned to call *Translation in Every Words (Tarjumeh beh zabān-i 'ālam va 'ādam)*. Taken together, these texts reveal a great poet and critic, as well as an original theorist of translation at work dissecting literary texts and probing their philosophical implications. Their style bears the heavy imprint of Elahi's two lodestars: Hölderlin and Rimbaud, whom he translated into Persian in 1973 and 1983, respectively. They also reveal an affinity with the American poet Ezra Pound, whose translation method Elahi discusses in the third selection. Although Pound is primarily known as a pioneering literary theorist and poet who effectively linked literary modernism to the practice of translation, his writing also bears the imprint of antisemitism and others racisms, as well as an attraction to Mussolini's fascism. Elahi however does not touch on any of these dimensions of Pound's politics; his interest is with Pound as a translator of Chinese poetry.

To an even greater degree than Hölderlin and Rimbaud, Elahi's writing is marked by various forms of interrupted speech, including ellipses and quotations. Like poetry, this feature of Elahi's prose creates a jarring effect in Persian, which we have endeavoured to reproduce in our translation. Elahi's ideas about translation jar even more than his prose. He considers translation as "a re-creation (*bāz-āfarinish*) even more difficult than the original" and adds that "if creation (*āfarinish*) is viewed as a dance, translation is a dance in chains." Elahi's striking metaphor of translation as a dance in chains is also reflected in his description of translation as a creative process

# MY SCENT THAT DOESN'T PASS

Be my metaphor in this inscription,[13]
my scent that doesn't pass,
my gaze at the grass, that makes a metaphor.

There you sit
atop a stone lion.
The lion gazes calmly,
at the hill below.[14]

Figure 2: Stone Lion from Chaharmahal and Bakhtiari Province

---

13. The word used here for "inscription," ganjnameh (letter for the treasury), literally indicates a document that specifies the location of a hidden treasure. Taken as a proper noun, *Ganjnama* also refers to an ancient Iranian inscription praising the Zoroastrian God Ahura Mazda. The *Ganjnama* inscription is located near a famous stone lion that is also referenced in this poem.
14. Stone lions that in ancient Iranian culture signified tombstones, particularly among the Bakhtiyari people (see figure 2).

## بوی من که نمی‌آید

در این گنجنامه استعاره من باش ؛
بوی من که نمی‌آید ،
نظاره من به علف ، که استعاره میشود .

آنجا
تو بر سر شیری سنگی نشسته ای ،
و شیر که پایین نگاه میکند
به تپه ای آرام .

# WILD GRASS

In memory of green
it is green.
Never say it is green.

The grass greens to say
it can green.
Never say it greens.
Never in the ruins. Never in the garden.

Never say it's trapped, never say it's free.
Even on this roof, the grass trembles
in the wind.

Wild grass
is wild grass.
Otherwise, it's nameless.

## علف دیمی

به یاد سبزیست
که سبزست ،
نگو سبزست .

سبز میشود که بگوید
سبز میشود ،
نگو سبز میشود ،
نگو در خرابه ، نگو در باغ –

نه بگو بندی ، نه بگو آزاد –
بر همین بام هم یکی
باد میخورد آخر .

علف دیمی
علف دیمیست ،
نه به اسمی دیگر .

1
At that moment from idleness
you rest in the left chamber of my heart
until a creature passes
and picks you up,
as if you were an orphan.

The pain
is certainly gradual.
One day
it will squat
in the small neighboring grave

and remain
all year long.

۱
آن وقت از بلاتکلیفی
در حفره چپ قلبم به چرت میافتی
تا تو را طبیعتی
سر راهی
بردارد .

درد
بیگمان تدریجیست . -
یک روز
که در قبر کوچک بغلی
چمباتمه میزند

و یک سال
طول میکشد

3
*To That One*

Sparks, sparks:
this one is that one—
that one cannot be this.
At night, when each moment shimmers so
much that it shimmers not at all.
Your youth
went to grasses
that rustled and dreamed not ...

Now dreams
make me age.

2
*Il orra le chant du
Patre tout la vie.*
--Apollinaire[12]

Here,
the hand you stretch—
is it a shepherd's hand
or the grass of days?

Over there,
the weathercock
lies in the sun.

Light years
go grazing and never arrive.
They have no piper
following them.

---

12. This quotation, which translates as "All through life they'll herd the herdsman's song" is from Apollinaire's poem "Le Brasier" (1913), and is given in French in the original. The poem was originally part of a series entitled "Le Pyrée," which references, among other things, the ancient Zoroastrian fire temple. (Thanks to Dr. Emma Tyler, University of Birmingham, for this information).

۳
به آن یکی


شراره‌ها ، شراره‌ها :
این یکی خود آن یکیست .
آن یکی نیست این یکی . -
در شب ، که چنان برق برق می‌زند هر دم
که هر دم انگار نمی‌زند .


جوانی تو
مال علف‌هایی بود
که خش و خش می‌کردند و خواب نمی‌دیدند -


اکنون رویا
پیرم می‌کند .

۲

این ،
دستی که دراز می‌کنی ،
دست چوپانی‌ست
یا علف ایام ؟


رو به رو
می‌لمد در آفتاب
مرغ بادنما .


به چرا ،
می‌روند و نمی‌رسند
سال‌های نوری ، که ندارند
نی‌نوازی در دنبال .

5
After all, you are sleepless.
You are a long night and sleepless.
You are a day without a sunrise …

You were
flourishing.
Light of my eyes!
In the sun …

After all, once you must
have known
a deep thirst, once.
You must have made a mirage,
in the middle of the sea.

4
All of a sudden, I was shocked with the fear of
you tumbling from the high wall.
I bent to catch you, but saw
you hanging on the bushes.

The old spring
burst up dry,
in blossoms
wrapped in older curtains and
somewhat shabby.

*Il orra le chant du*
*Patre tout la vie.*
—Apollinaire

۵
با این همه خواب نداری
شبی درازی و خواب نداری
روزی و آفتاب نداری -

بی‌نیاز
تو بوده‌ای
نورِ چشم ! -
در آفتاب‌ها -

با این همه باید یک بار
یک تشنگی بلد
بوده باشی ، یک بار
یک سراب ساخته باشی
وسط دریا .

۴
یک‌باره ترس برم داشت
افتاده باشی از سر دیوار ،
خم شدم بگیرم دیدم
خوشه خوشه آویخته‌ای .

بهار قدیم
خشک بر آمد ،
با شکوفه‌ها
که در پرده‌های قدیم‌تر ماند و
اندکی چرک‌نما .

7
At dawn, your summit will turn scarlet
from your fear
from anything you have but
you don't have for fear …

Desire for air—that you don't breathe
in yet it breathes
in you—
is lovely blue.

You would fall.
You would rise.
And when amazed,
you would be my foothills.

6
Your absence does not shine
from the breath
that I hold.

I die like this—
alive.
Like this. Sunless,
you are bright,

O Reza's turquoise![11]

---

11. Reza's turquoise has multiple significations in Persian. Most directly, it refers to the turquoise tiles in the shrine (*haram*) of Imam Reza in Mashhad (where this section of the poem was composed in 1349/ 1970). The entire poem can be seen as a rendering of the death of the speaker who holds their breath while this holy turquoise is illuminated even in the absence of the sun (and while pointing to the tiles before the sunny brilliance of the gold dome of Imam Reza). At the same time, reza is also an adjective meaning "happy," or "satisfied," in the absence of a proper name as referent. Hence this line can also be translated as "Happy turquoise!"

۷
و سحر، قله‌های تو را سرخ‌تر
کند ترس
که از هر چه داری و
از ترس خود نمی‌داری -

که هوای هواست - که دم
درو نمی‌زنی و
در تو می‌زند -
آبی‌ی دوست‌داشتنی .

بیفتی
بلند شوی
و بهتت که می‌زند
دامنه‌هایم باشی .

۶
از نفسی
که حبس می‌کنم ، نه که غیبت تو
بدرخشد ..

چنینه می‌میرم
از زند گی ،
چنینه که بی آفتاب
روشنی ،

فیروزه‌ی رضا !

# SONG OF THE MOON HANGING OVER THE FIELDS OF DAMASCUS[10]

The fields grow grass
destined for oblivion.
And grass reminds you of the fields.
How generous are the grassless fields!

How do you assume your burning
will last forever, o Damascus moon?
At last, light
quenches the flames in
the wildfire. Love.

The morning star
knows where you end.
It knows and is ignorant.

8
You peep through each reed-bed.
Yet you are not the moon.

I am acquainted with black insects
that become the moonlight
for fear of
the moonlight.

---

10. The title for this poem puns on the meaning of *mu'allaqā*, which carries the sense of hanging, and the *Mu'allaqāt*, a series of Arabic poems that hung in the Ka'ba in pre-Islamic Mecca, before the city became a holy site within Islam. In modern Farsi, *mu'allaqā* also means "upside-down"; hence the poem is "upside-down."

## معلقه‌ی ماه روی دشتهای دمشق

و دشت‌ها که سبزه می‌رویند
تا فراموش شوند ،
اما از سبزه دشت یاد می‌آید
ای فتا ، دشت‌های بی‌سبزه !

از چه این سوزش را
همیشه پنداری ؟. - ای ماه دمشق !
و نورست آخر
که می‌نشاند آتش را در
حریق جنگل‌ها . - عشق .

ستاره‌ی سحری
می‌داند کجا می‌انجامی .
می‌داند ، و نمی‌داند .

۸
رخ بیرون می‌گذاری از هر نیزار
گرچه ماه نیستی . -

و می‌شناسم حشراتی سیاه
که مهتاب می‌شوند ،
بس که می‌ترسند
از مهتاب .

# THE CROW'S SONNET

*Thank God! We got rid of the battle.*
—Rumi

        It is neither strange
        nor fun
        when they knock on the door.
        You see it's a crow that says:
        *Damn this forgetfulness.*
        *Always dig and hide, always search and find one.*
        *The worm-eaten one, shit, damn—*
        *damn this forgetfulness.*

        Damn this forgetfulness.
        This ridiculous truth, this spiritless song
        will not touch me
        in any way at all.

# غزل کلاغ

المنهٔ لله که ز پیکار رهیدیم
مولوی

عجیب نیست
مسخره نیست
در که میزنند
ببنید کلاغیست ، بگوید
امان از این فراموشی
هی بکن قایم کن ، هی بگرد پیدا کنی یکی
آن هم این کرمخورده ، تف ، امان
امان از این فراموشی

امان از این فراموشی
که این حقیقت مضحک ، که این تغنی بیروح
یاد من نمی‌آید
به هیچ وجه من الوجوه .

# TIGER

You, imprisoned by this simile!
Leap! Boy! Rip!

Bars, my dear, are verses.
They soar when you flee.

For an instant, you turn pale
and sober, in papery air.

# ببر

زندانی این تشبیه !
بپر ، پسر ، بدر !

میله ها ، نازنین ، ابیاتند ،
میپرند اگر بپری ،

یک آن که سفید میشوی ، هشیار ،
در هوای کاغذوار .

# EAGLE

That bird on top of the mountain
who has built a house
cannot be distinguished
from the perpetual snow.
*Come! Come!* He says,
*Why don't you come here?*
He knows that no one can ascend. He knows.
He knows that I will collapse on the way.
He wants exactly this
to come lift me up
and color me white as snow.

# عقاب

آن پرنده که بالای کوه
خانه ساخته ،
از برف همیشگی
نمیشود شناخته .
میگوید بیا ، بیا ،
چرا نیایی اینجا؟
میداند نمیشود به پا آمد ، میداند .
میداند میان راه میافتم ،
او هم این را میخواهد -
تا بیاید مرا بلند کند ،
ببرد آن بالا ، رنگِ برف کند .

# WHAT YOU HAVE READ SO FAR

I said: I have received a letter. It ordered me,
at such and such a date and such and such a place,
to join another group
and move to city B.
The letter's author was unknown.
I checked an atlas, and could not find city B.
Two days later, my friend, Raha
passed away tragically.
He had received the same letter just before he died
he had said the night before
he had dreamed of a bird,
resembling a hoopoe.
The next day this bird
entered my dream.
I therefore had to join the same group at the stated place.
I said: We were roughly thirty people.
We began our journey.
Along the way
an old man named Allahyar joined us.
We will see what a major role he has.
So a few days later, another group who said
passed that valley. They assumed we were their group
but were supposed to join a different group.
Were we were nearing
the city B
which was nowhere
on the map?
We have reached here.
Anxious of the gradual increase, Allahyar says:
Something must be done, and quickly.
What can be done with this crowd of Laylis
and this herd of men?
And here the story begins …

## تا اینجا که خوانده‌اید

گفتم نامه‌یی به من رسیده حکم کرده بود
تا به تاریخ فلان و فلان جا باید
به جمع دیگری پیوسته
به شهر ب حرکت کنیم.
نامه را که نوشته بود معلوم نبود، مع‌هذا،
با رجوع به اطلس، شهری به نام ب نیافتم.
دو روز بعد دوستم رها
به وضع اسفناکی درگذشت:
عین نامه به او هم رسیده بود و قبل از آن که بمیرد
گفته بود شب
مرغی به خوابش آمده بود،
چیزی انگار شکل شانه به سر.
روز بعد پرنده‌ی مذکور
به خواب من آمد و
این بود که مجبور شدم در مکان مقرر به همان جمع بپیوندم

گفتم حدود سی نفری
حرکت کردیم،
میان راه
پیرمردی به نام اللهیار به ما پیوست،
که خواهیم دید در آینده چه نقش مهمی دارد.
چند روز بعد هم جمع دیگری که گفتند
قرار است پشت آن دره به جمع دیگری بپیوندند
و در اول خیال کرده بودند ما همان جمعیم.
آیا به این قرار
به شهر ب
که در نقشه نبود
نزدیک می‌شدیم؟
به این جا رسیده‌ایم که اللهیار،
نگران از ازدیاد تدریجی‌ی جمعیت، می‌گوید:
باید، هر چه زودتر، فکری کرد -
با این گله‌ی لیلی، با یک شهر نره خر،
چه کاری از پیش می‌رود؟ -
و حال دنباله‌ی ماجرا -

# FOR TWO WEEKS I HAVE BEEN IN THIS PALACE, NOTHING HAS HAPPENED[9]

Baghdad's arches and the arches of the Tigris—
The story left unfinished
may turn into a poem and a poem
finished     can make a story. That's why poets
always break the lines of their poems. And I want
from among those pointless walks around Baghdad
to break the line on a house in the bazaar
carpeted with many marbled stones in *The Thousand and one Nights*,
where the ceilings
are painted turquoise and gold.
*Ten dinars a month for rent!*
*Are you kidding?*
*I'm not kidding,* the doorkeeper said, *but whoever enters the house*
*gets sick and within two weeks dies.*
For two weeks
I've been in this palace and nothing has happened.
I've only seen sunsets of gold.
You can hear them:
*Hey, boy, you haven't seen the palace belvedere?* the doorkeeper's wife said.
But what is on the roof
other than Baghdad's arches and the arches of the Tigris—

---

9. This poem offers a poetic retelling of a story in the Arabic *A Thousand and One Nights*, "The House and the Belvedere" (night 599). Elahi's poem reproduces the phrasing of the Persian translation of *A Thousand and One Nights* by 'Abd al-Latif Tasuji Tabrizi (1858)..

## یکی دو هفته میشود که توی این قصرم و هیچ اتفاق نیافتاده

تاق‌های ضربی‌ی بغداد و تاق‌های ضربی دجله ...
قصه اگر ناتمام می‌ماند
یحتمل که شعر می‌شد و شعر
در تمامیّتِ خود قصه می‌شود . به همین دلیل ، شاعران
همیشه ، جخت ، تقطیع می‌کنند و من می‌خواهم
از آن گشت‌های بی‌حوصله در بغداد
تقطیع کنم روی خانه‌یی در بازار
که ، در الف لیل ، زمینش را
گونه گونه رخام گسترده‌اند و سقف‌های غرفه‌ها
به لاجورد و آب زر نقش کرده‌اند :
اجرتش ماهی دَه دینار !
واقعاً راسته با مسخره‌ام می‌کنید ؟ دربان گفت :
واقعاً راسته امّا که هر توی خانه بیاید
یکی دو هفته بیشتر نمی‌کشد مریض می‌شود می‌میرد .
یکی دو هفته می‌شود
که توی قصرم و هیچ اتفاق نیافتاده است ؛
فقط غروب‌ها طلایی‌ست : می‌شود شنفت !
واقعاً چه غفلتی ! پسرم ! مگر هنوز
به بام قصر نرفته‌ای ؟ زنِ دربان گفت .
مگر از بام قصر چیست
جز همین تاق‌های ضربی‌ی بغداد و تاق‌های ضربی‌ی دجله ...

# DOULEUR D'APRÈS DOYLE

They are ringing all the time: Sir,
a thing has happened that must not have happened. Then
they make an appointment. But
no one can find the cursed door.
No one knows
it opens onto the yard,
to a walnut tree and crows hidden
in no one knows where in this damned world.
Here, where you always sit, stir the tea, and watch
the clouds that
grow perpetually and shrink
and so minute by minute it seems
they are dancing with time.
Sometimes by accident in the evenings
it seems that you have missed something, then
you realise that it was due to the lack of light when that
old friend
turns on the lamp: Hello, Holmes, why
do you sit in darkness?

## DOULEUR D'APRÉS DOYLE

دائماً زنگ می‌زنند - آقا ،
آنچه نباید بشود شده . بعد
قرار ملاقات می‌گذارند . اما
در بی‌صاحب را که هیچ کس نمی‌یابد ،
که هیچ کس نمی‌داند
که باز می‌شود به حیاط ،
به یک درخت گردوی گرده‌ها کلاغ‌ها نهفته در نمی‌دانم
کجاهای این سرِ دنیای کوفتی .
این‌جا که همیشهَ می‌نشینیّ و چای هم می‌زنیّ و به ابرها
نگاه می‌کنی
که دائماً بزرگ می‌شوند و کوچک و اینقدر ، خلاصه ،
دقیقه دقیقه که
انگار
با زمان می‌رقصند .
گاهی اتفاق میافتد غروب‌ها
چیزی انگار گمت شده باشد ، بعد
می‌بینی از نبودِ نور بوده وقتی آن رفیق قدیمی
کلید چراغ را می‌زند - سلام استاد ، چرَا
در تاریکی نشسته‌ای ؟

# DUPIN DETECTS[8]

The other one had a spot on his forehead,
The plan was perfect: a hole through the ceiling …
and the moon in eclipse …
Both had broken in.
Then everywhere flashed white.
Dazzling, from without and within.
We are in doubt. Otherwise it would be simpler.
Perhaps the gem's dazzling
was beyond depicting, or perhaps
the landlord had turned on the light without warning.
Each thief's position was fixed.
The landlord was in place. All was fixed, fixed by light
here, in this room, so simply furnished: a table
and on the shelf,
a statue of Shiva.
In a picture,
at the beginning of our detection, white, absolutely white
…
We are in doubt. Was it over-exposed?
Did they open
the damn camera up
in a lighted place instead of a darkroom,
or was no photo taken at all?

---

8. The title occurs in English in Elahi's Persian text. C. Auguste Dupin is a fictional character created by Edgar Allan Poe, and a prototype for the detective story genre.

# DUPIN DETECTS

آن یکی خال به پیشانی داشت ،
نقشه هم دقیق بود : حفره‌ای در سقف –
و ماه در خسوف –
هر دو تو آمده بودند ولی بعد فضای سفید بود ،
خیرگی شده بود از درون
یا بیرون ،
حتم نداریم و گرنه ساده‌تر می‌بود :
شاید برق جواهر بیرون
از حد تصور بود ، یا شاید
صاحبخانه غفلتاً کلید چراغ را زده بود .
هر دزد ، به جا ، ثابت شد ،
صاحبخانه به جا و ثبوت این همه ، باری ، ثبوت نور شد
این‌جا ، در این اتاق – با این اثاث ساده : یک میز
و روی قفسه
یک مجسمه شیوا –
در عکسی ،
نقطه شروع ردیابی‌ی ما ، سفید ، واقعا سفید سفید –
و حتم نداریم که از نوردیدگی‌ست ،
که دوربین بی‌صاحب را
جای تاریکخانه در فضای نورانی
باز کرده‌اند ، یا از اصل
عکسی نگرفته بودند .

# STATIONS

I.

I was your slave
between thirty pasts and ten futures
One half of me became a shadow,
a shadow spread by laurels
at the bottom of the valley.
Where the shameless light is wounded by your sanctum,
seven quiet balsams, seven balsams of shadow
And the prayer beneath the lip—
was I and—alas—myself.
I, your servant,
saw only your navel and not even your navel.
I lie, facing your threshold
Between ten pasts and thirty futures.
The moon beside my face
is the light's dying gasp.
I'm not cold anymore.
A blanket is enough for me.

# مقدمه

۱

دردره

من غلام تو بودم . –
و میانِ سی گذشته و ده آینده ،
یک نیمه‌ی من سایه شد ؛
سایه که بر گهای بو
ته دره می‌گرایانند .
جا که نورِ گستاخ
از حریمِ تو زخم خورده ، هفت مرهم آهسته ، هفت مرهم سایه
،
و دعای زیر لب که
من بودم و ، آه ، من خودم .
من ، غلام تو ، اما ،
تنها نافِ تو را دیدم ، و نه حتا
نافِ تو را .
اما دراز ، رو به درگاهِ تو می‌کشم ،
میانِ ده گذشته و سی آینده ،
و ماه کنار صورتم
پتپتی دارد .
... دیگر سردم نیست ،
یک ملافه‌هم کافی‌ست .

## DISSECTING AN ONION

Without core, instead
labyrinthine.
What is a core,
if not the relation of the layers?

Centerless circles spiraling out
cut their relationships.

It is high tide of the eyes.

## تشریح پیاز

بی‌مغز ، در عوضِ تو در تو .
مغز ، اما ، چیست
جز روابطِ تویه‌ها ؟

گشودنِ دوایرِ بی‌مرکز
آشفتنِ رابطه‌هاست ....

و مدِّ بینایی .

## AND WHO?

And who saw the year
was born with so many violets?
when thirst
was sweet.

You won't keep me away from your memory.
I wasted my youth – lovely skin!
Meanwhile, another youth
is grafted onto you.

In this place, several violets were enough
to cover the well's mouth.

## اما که

اما که دید سال
با چند بنفشه به دنیا آمد؟ —
کی که تشنگی
شیرین بود.

دورم از یاد نمی‌داری:
به هدر رفته جوانیم —
پوستی شگرف - اما
چسبیده به تو، جوانی دیگر!

این‌جا که بسنده بود
چند بنفشه به پوشاندن دهانه چاه.

# ALONE –

Nothing will you gain.
Nothing will you lose.
Only a streak of blood,
only a way
to avoid experience.
Red but
from the lovers' mistakes.
You don't even gain.
You don't even lose.
The white butterfly
slowly sinks
into the wine of your age.

# تنها ـ

چیزی به دست نمی آری ،
چیزی نمی‌دهی از دست ؛
تنها خطی خون ،
تنها راهی برای اجتناب
از واقع ،
سرخ ، اما
از اشتباه عاشقان .
حتا به دست نمی آری ،
حتا نمی‌دهی از دست ،
بس که آهسته غرق می‌شود
پروانه سفید
در شراب سن تو

# From Vision
## دیدن

2.

Oh, my friend! My friend!
Twice is enough.
The third is spring air.
When Icarus falls
from the green sky
The narcissus' corolla fills with rainwater.
Look inside: a small Icarus
ascends.


V.
### From Icarus and the Bondsman of the Deer[7]

Just as the thunderstorm in the rainbow
mixes colors with colors
I wish that poetry could mix the two legends together
so that we could stare at each other in the poison sunrise,
and the plants would recognise water in the poison sunrise.
(Water is our majestic sacrifice and has taught them
the secret of life and us the secret of death.)
And the sun would fit into the grape.
(The grape is the Holy Last Supper.)
Now that the flood of sun has taken the wing away,
the deer is helpless.
He falls.
Generous deer bestow nothing.
They watch and watch and watch.
Now that the sun slowly
moves west
on the hill, two fires have turned red.
The horizon is recognised in your compromise.
This horizon of bliss: the bondsman of water
concealed in wet firewood

---

7. "Deer Bondsman" is a title for the eighth Shia Imam, Reza (766-819). Reza's name, meaning 'bliss', is referenced in the second to last line. According to legend, Imam Reza protected a deer from being killed by a hunter. He died after being poisoned by grapes. The two legends to which the poet refers are those of Imam Reza and Icarus.

آه، ای یار! ای یار!
دوبار تکرار، بس است
که سومین، هوای بهاری‌ست.
آن دم که از آسمان سبز
ایکار، سقوط می‌کند،
جام نرگس پر باران است
و در آن ـ ببین! ـ ایکاری کوچکتر
عروج می‌کند.


از ایکار و ضامن آهو


چنین که رگبار، در قوس قزح
رنگ در رنگ می‌آمیزد،
کاش که شعر، می‌توانست دو افسانه را به هم آمیزد:
تا که ما، در طلوع سم، به هم نظاره کنیم
تا گیاهان، در طلوع سم، آب را به جای آرند
(آب که ایثار بزرگ ماست، و به آنان
راز زندگی، و به ما راز مرگ را گفته‌ست.)
و خورشید در دانه‌ی انگور بگنجد؛
(انگور که شام آخر قدسی‌ست.)
اما اکنون که سیل خورشید، بال را برده‌ست
از آهوان هیچ ساخته نیست.
او، می‌افتد
و آهوان سخی هیچ نمی‌بخشند
جز نظاره، نظاره، نظاره.
و اکنون که آفتاب، ارام آرام،
به غرب می‌رود،
دو تش، بر تپه سرخ شده‌اند،
و در سازش تو، افق شناخته می‌شود
افق رضا: ضامن آب پنهان هیزم تر
که به آتش گذاشته‌اند.

III. Icaruses

The word with its movement—the word in flight—
has filled the space with the scent of flesh.
What is a poem but the movement of a word?

In the room the women
are talking of Icarus
while Icarus' poem
is not composed.

Just one word:
the sun!

And if you return someday
from that burning pilgrimage,
I will fill the torches cup by cup with the sea
and you will know that its flame
is the bluest and coldest of flames.


IV. In Reverse

*to Mohsen Sabā*

1.

The one who left will never return
will collapse.
At the cloud the narcissus stares at the cloud.
It rains. It does not rain.
Beneath the wet cloak,
when will I be moved to bring the firewood?

---

6  Mohsen Saba (d. 2018) was a friend Bijan Elahi and author of *Du Guftar (Two Narratives; Tehran: Avanevesht, 2015), a memoir that recounts his friendships with Bijan Elahi and Jalal Al-e Ahmad.*

## ایکارها

کلمه با حرکت خود -کلمه، به پرواز-
فضا را از عطر گوشت آکنده‌ست.
پس به جز حرکت یک کلمه، شعر چیست؟

زنان در اتاق
از ایکار سخن می‌گویند،
لیک، شعر ایکار
ساخته
نمی‌شود.
فقط یک کلمه:
خورشید!

وز آن زیارت سوزان
روزی اگر باز آیید،
دریا را، کاسه کاسه، در مشعل‌ها می‌ریزم
تا بدانید شعله‌اش
آبی‌ترین و سردترین شعله‌ست.

## بالعکس

۱

آن که رفت، بازنمی‌گردد،
می‌افتد.
نرگس، به ابر خیره‌ست، به ابر.
باران می‌بارد، لیک نمی‌بارد.
زیر شنلی مرطوب
پس کی وحی می‌رسد که هیزمی بردارم؟

# FIVE SCENES FROM ICARUS

I. Justice

Each word
is sacrificed to a sword
that beams forth its light.
It rains.
Each word wears a white mask
and a self to be
submitted to the rain.
Each word is an angel
trembling from nakedness.

I have lifted the sword.
I rip the mask
off the word
and place it on my face.
I submit myself
to the rain
and before the scent of life ascends,
I take flight
with the angel's two wings.

The rain has stopped.
The sun of language
draws near!

II. Misty Dreams

The sky wanted
a misty sip from me
when the hood of the stroller filled with dew.
In the stroller, sleep seized you.

Through the vineyard, through the mist,
slumber and wine were distributed.
Cheers
in the mist!

Icarus
fell.

## پنج مجلس از ایکار

### عدالت

هر کلمه
فدای شمشیری‌ست
که در او رخشان است.
باران می‌بارد.
در هر کلمه نقابی‌ست سفید،
جانی‌ست تا به باران
تسلیم شود.
هر کلمه فرشته‌یی‌ست
که از عریانی می‌لرزد.

شمشیر را به دست گرفته‌ام
نقاب را
درمی‌آرم از کلمه
به رخسار می‌زنم،
جان به باران
تسلیم می‌کنم،
و هنوز عطر عمر برنخاسته،
با دو بال فرشته
پر می‌گیرم.

باران بند آمده‌ست،
خورشید زبان
چه نزدیک است.

### خاب‌های مه

جرعه‌یی مه گرفته
از من آسمان می‌خاست
که سقف کالسکه پر از شبنم شد.
در کالسکه، تو را خاب در ربود.
از تاکستان، از میان مه،
خاب را، با شراب، پیش آوردند.
در مه،
بسلامتی!

و ایکار
افتاد.

4.
Here
is that bird in mirrors.
Let us break the mirrors!
Shall the bird die
or shall it be born?
An image born
is a mirror broken
A mirror dead
is an image broken.

5.
*Fable*

A bird
lived in a mirror.
The mirror
broke.
The mirror birthed a bird.
The bird
melted the mirror,
drank the water,
and became a mirror.

6.
Here I am, having become
the bird in the mirror.

۴
و اینك
آن پرنده در آینه‌هاست.
آینه‌ها را بشکنیم!
پرنده خواهد مرد
یا زاده خواهد شد؟
تولد تصویر
شکست آینه‌هاست
مرگ آینه‌ها
شکست تصویرهاست.

۵
قصه

پرنده‌ای
در آینه می‌زیست
آینه
شکست:
پرنده‌اش را زاد.
پرنده
آینه را آب کرد،
آب را نوشید:
آینه شد!

۶
و من
پرنده‌ی این آینه شدم.

# MOURNING THE BIRTH OF IMAGE

1.
Time
turned blue.
Your fingers brought no more good news.
Your fingers used to be a ladder
on which plucked doves
would climb to the roof.

2.
Time
turned blue.
And in its veins
there lived another time
that struck his heart at the glass
and tore the newborn hour
in pieces.

3.
Suddenly
in the father's veins,
I was out of breath,
a sperm who dreamed of a mother
for years.[5]
The mother
was searching for a bird
in the tree's veins.
She had forgotten
the bird's empty perch
on the branch.

---

5 - The same Persian word—mani—here denotes both the first-person pronoun "I" and sperm.

## زاری بر تولد تصویر

۱
زمان
به کبودی می‌گرایید
دیگر با انگشتانت بشارتی نبود!
انگشتانت که نردبامی بود
تا کبوتران پر کنده
به بام برآیند.

۲
زمان
به کبودی می‌گرایید
و در رگ‌هایش
زمانی دیگر می‌زیست
که قلبش را بر شیشه‌ها می‌کوفت
و نوزاد ساعت را
تکه تکه می‌کرد.

۳
ناگهان
در رگهای پدر
«من»ی به سختی نفس نفس زد
«من»ی که سال‌ها
خواب مادر می‌دید.
و مادر
در رگ‌های یک درخت
به دنبال پرنده‌ای می‌گشت
و جای خالی پرنده را
بر شاخ
از یاد برده بود.

They grew me,
grew me to surround me
by hasty suns.
You passed and picked me so smoothly
that I touched the breeze
in your hands.
You witnessed the sun and the air,
with breeze in your burning red hair.
The water beasts
went to sleep quietly
and each one of them touched
your clear blood
In their dreams.
You became a face
I gazed at
and
gaze at.
Like a new birth, my love is
still slime and blood.

Come
for indeed the small yards
will be covered by insects and light.
I laugh for you.

I laugh for you.
The black locust
receives us today
with cool evening drink.

مرا کاشته بودند
کاشته بودندم تا با خورشیدهای عجول
احاطه‌ام کنند.
تو آمدی و چنان نرم مرا چیدی
که رفتار نسیم را در دست تو حس کردم.
تو شاهد خورشید و هوا شدی
نسیم در گیسوان سرخ سوزانت.
جانوران آرام به خواب شدند
و رفتار خون صافی‌ی تو
در خواب یکایکشان
حس شد.
تو مانند چهره‌یی شدی
که من بر او نگریستم
و
می‌نگرم.
عشقم چون تولدی تازه
هنوز لزج و خونی‌ست.
بیا
حیاط‌های کوچک را
حشرات و نور می‌پوشانند.
برای تو می‌خندم.

برای تو می‌خندم.
اقاقیا
امروز برایمان
شربت خنک عصرانه می‌آرد.

# I LAUGH FOR YOU

The black locust,[4] angel of the poor
is preparing for us
her cool evening drink.
I bend towards you:
your skin
moves like breeze and water beasts.
The air is a cup of the spirit
of a burning and witnessing moth
between a thousand suns and a thousand shadows of you.

You are the white corn husks of my childhood
that I glean again.
You are my first fingers.
The poor laugh
beside green cucumber bushes.
Do you see how naked I am?
My umbilical cord is uncut.
Like a new birth, my love is
slime and blood.
I laugh for you.

The houses nearby
are lit earlier.
The air between thousands of lamps
and thousands of your shadows near and far
rises in ash.

---

4 - Technically known as *Robinia pseudoacacia* (Persian *aqaqiya*), this tree, found on many streets in Tehran, is also called the false acacia and the black locust. Its flowers are used to make a drink for those who cannot afford cold drinks.

## برای تو می‌خندم

اقاقیا فرشته فقرا
شربت عصرانه خنکش را
برایمان مهیا می‌سازد.

بر تو خم می‌شوم:
رفتار نسیم و جانوران آب
در پوست توست.
و هوا جام جان شاپرکی‌ست
که در میان هزار خورشید و هزار سایه‌ی تو
می‌سوزد و شاهد است.

تو خوشه‌های سپید خردسالی‌ی منی
که دوباره می‌چینم.
تو انگشتان نخستین منی.
کنار جالیزهای سبز خیار
فقرا می‌خندند:
می‌بینی چگونه برهنه‌ام؛
حتا ناف مرا هنوز نبریده‌اند:
عشقم چون تولدی تازه
هنوز لزج و خونی‌ست.
برای تو می‌خندم.

در خانه‌های نزدیک
چراغ‌ها را زودتر افروخته‌اند.
هوا میان هزاران چراغ و هزاران سایه‌ی تو
از دوردست تا نزدیک
خاکستر است.

# TASSEOGRAPHY III[3]

There was a time when
before the cups were
turned upside down[2]
when futures were wide open
and life moved
in forms beyond itself.

---

3 - During tasseography, cups are turned upside down in extract coffee grains from the bottom and to predict the future on that basis.

# فال قهوه ۳

زمانی
پیش از آن که فنجان‌ها را وارون کنند
آینده‌ها گشوده بود
و زندگی در قالبی ماورای خود شکل می‌گرفت .

# TASSEOGRAPHY II

A willow tree in life,
with white veins in red streams
(and not bloody crimson),
is a ship's journey.
A man faces sunrise.
A woman faces sunset,
leaning back to back.
The sea intersects their faces
on this ship's journey.

## فال قهوه ۳

درخت بید در زندگی
رگ‌های سفید به جوبار سرخ
(و این سرخی خون نیست)
سفر با کشتی
مردی که طلوع می‌بیند
زنی که غروب
از پشت به هم تکیه دادند
بین چهره‌هاشان دریاست
سفر با کشتی .

# TASSEOGRAPHY I[2]

A small mouse
in your hand,
a pretty mouse
with bright eyes
heads toward sweet crimson.

(A bit later
you will be heartless.)

---

2- Tasseography *(fal giri)* is to the practice of predicting the future on the basis of coffee grounds (or related materials), a widespread practice in Iran. The collected poetry *(diwan)* of Hafez was also consulted in this manner. Each episode in this poem involves a specific method through which the future was read from material remnants.

## فال قهوه ۱

یک موش کوچک
یک موش زیبا
با چشمانی روشن
در دست تو
به سوی قرمزی‌های شیرین

(اندکی بعد
قلب نداری.)

# BIRTHPLACE

All these roads would end in white
if they replied to you.

Your birthplace, you knew, was a town
bigger than your heart
that left you without an answer.

A woman's lips blossoms
in a town smaller than hearts.
A woman's lips end in white,
to the cold cheeks of the year's martyrs,
my cold cheek was a sun
that did not reply.

## زادگاه

این همه راه به سپیدی می‌رسید
اگر به تو پاسخ می‌دادند .

تو شهری را زادگاه خود دانستی
که از دلت بزرگتر بود
و تو را بی‌پاسخ گذاشت .

لب‌های زنی به گل می‌نشیند
در شهری کوچکتر از دل‌ها .
لب‌های زنی به سپیدی می‌رسد
با گونه‌های سرد شهدای سال
با گونه‌های سرد من
که خورشید بی‌پاسخ روز بود .

# I BELIEVED

Before cocks crowed
I believed
your eyelids
opened dawn's book.

Your mouth held for me
laughter warmer than the unrisen sun,
than the tear, again to be shed.
The cocks fell asleep before they crowed.
They understood they would have other days to crow.
They knew they would be forgiven
when the end comes for us all.

I believed.
I swear by young dreams that I believed
the innocence of your eyelids,
the innocence of leaves,
whitened in light.
I swear by all that is white.

Only the cypress betrayed.
It was courted by every season.

## باور کردم

پیش از صدای خروسان
باور کردم
که پلک‌های تو
کتاب صبح را گشود .

از آفتابی که نیامده بود
از اشک که باید دوباره ریخت
دهانت برای من خنده‌های گرمتر داشت .
و خروسان پیش از صدای خود دوباره به خواب شدند
از این که پذیرفتند روزها دیگر با ماست
و این که تا روز مرگ بخشیده شدند
تا پایانی که ما نیز با آن خواهیم بود

باور کردم
سوگند به خواب‌های جوان باور کردم
بی‌گناهی پلک‌های تو را
بی‌گناهی برگ‌ها را
که در نور سپید شدند
سوگند به هر چه سپیدی‌ست

تنها سرو خیانت کرد
که پذیرفته‌ی همه فصل‌ها بود

# From youths

# جوانی‌ها

We have also included our translation of Elahi's scattered writings on the theory and practice of translation. Not included here are Elahi's numerous and highly innovative translations from the major poets of world literature (see Further Reading for a list of his translations). Each of these translations deserves to be studied on its own terms, by scholars versed in the source and target languages, and it is hoped that future generations will bring to light the uniqueness of Elahi's legacy as a poet and translator who reconceptualized the boundaries between writing and translation. All footnotes in the poems below, as well as in our translation of Elahi's prose, have been added by us.

Figure 1: Tomb of Elahi at New Bijdeh. Photograph by Kayvan Tahmasebian.

mind and the collection never appeared. Fifty-One Publishing House was soon thereafter banned, allegedly by the Shah.

Elegant, meditative, and experimental, Elahi's poetry offers an unprecedented synthesis of the Persian classical poetic styles with the modernism he inherited from Nima Yushij (1895-1960), widely regarded as the founder of modernist Persian poetry, and best known for his formal innovations. Simultaneously, he absorbed world poetry through his renowned translations of Federico Garcia Lorca, T. S. Eliot, Hallaj, Henri Michaux, Pablo Neruda, Arthur Rimbaud, Constantine Cavafy, and Friedrich Hölderlin, among many other major writers. Apart from his innovations that broke new ground in modernist Persian literature, Elahi's poems are notable for their heterogeneity of forms and themes. His poetry synthesizes old and new, oriental and occidental, religious and secular, and formal and informal, offering a taste of the modernizing mysticism that informed both his personal life and his writing. Elahi crafts into a sophisticated and estranged language a modernist take on the multifaceted legacy of classical Persian poetry: Sa'eb's farfetched flights of imagination, Rumi's passionate lyricism, Khaqani's enigmatic and erudite compositions, Hafez's fragmented subject. He also effects a modernist compromise between the lucid naturalism of Nima Yushij and Shamlu's elegant archaism.

The poetic ambitions of the New Wave poetry of the 1960s generation in Iran were soon drowned out by voices of the revolution that dominated the political and social fervor of 1979, such as Khosro Golsorkhi (executed in 1974) and Saeed Soltanpour (executed in 1981). The 1979 revolution was followed by a decade long war between Iran and Iraq that left no room for or interest in the detached aesthetics of Other Poetry, and which witnessed a turn away from poetry that treated art as a value in itself. Buried, in accordance with his will, in New Bijdeh, a small village perched on the isolated heights of Alborz Mountains in northern Iran, Elahi's specter haunts Persian poetry today even more visibly than it did during his lifetime. The distinguished Iranian literary critic Qassem Hasheminejad attests that with Elahi's death, "the Persian language lost a considerable portion of its capabilities...[Elahi] was the most important, the most talented and the most wide-ranging literary figure of the last three decades."

This bilingual edition gathers together twenty poems from Elahi's two posthumously published collections, *Vision* (2014) and *Youths* (2015). Our translations are based mostly on the Bidgol Publication's editions, although in some cases we have reverted to the first version of Elahi's poem.

# Introducing Bijan Elahi

Bijan Elahi, the poet whose works are translated here in book form for the first time, was born in 1945 to a wealthy family in Tehran. Elahi studied painting under the guidance of the Iranian painter Javad Hamidi, with two of his paintings accepted for the Paris biennale, before devoting himself exclusively to poetry. For much of his life, Elahi was the leading figure in a circle of young poets who developed the movement known as Other Poetry (she'r-e digar), which was to transform Iranian literary modernism during the 1960s and 1970s. Other Poetry was itself the inheritor of the New Wave poetry movement that marked the highlight of avant-garde poetics in pre-revolutionary Iran.

Although one of the most erudite poets of his lifetime, Elahi never completed a formal education. He took leave of public life early in his career, spending his final three decades immersed in Sufism and poetic creation and translation in his home in northern Tehran. During the last three decades of his life, Elahi neither published his poems nor appeared in public. His work entered the public spotlight after his death from a heart attack in 2010. The young generation of contemporary Iranian poets have turned to Elahi's verse as a vehicle for new modes of expression and experimentation.

Elahi's poems were posthumously published in two volumes, from which our translations have been drawn: Vision (2014) and Youths (2015). Youths brings together what the poet's calls his "young poems," many of which had been published in serial form prior to the 1979 revolution. Vision is a collection of four poem cycles that indicate the fullness of Elahi's contribution to Persian literature.

As a perfectionist unwilling to publish his work in the intellectual climate of Pahlavi Iran and indifferent to fame, Elahi cancelled the distribution of nearly all the two hundred copies of the poem cycle *The Dross of The Days,* which had been scheduled for publication in 1972. The publisher for this cycle, Fifty-One Publishing House, was an avant-garde publisher managed by the film and literary critic Shamim Bahar, who later became Elahi's literary executor. The press was best known for its volumes on noted directors such as Pier Paolo Pasolini, Federico Fellini, and Stanley Kubrick. Elahi later also made preparations for the publication of a full collection of poems, entitled *Vision* and including *The Dross of The Days,* by this same publisher. Yet he changed his

# Table of Contents

1. Introducing Bijan Elahi

2. From *Youths* (جوانی‌ها)

   I Believed/ باور کردم
   Birthplace/ زادگاه
   Tasseography I, II, III/ فال قهوه
   I Laugh for You/ برای تو می‌خندم
   Mourning the Birth of Image/ زاری بر تولد تصویر
   Five Scenes from Icarus/ پنج مجلس از ایکار

3. From *Vision* (دیدن)

   Alone/ تنها
   And Who?/ اما که؟
   Dissecting an Onion/ تشریح پیاز
   Stations/ مقامه
   Dupin Detects/ Dupin Detects
   Douleur d'Après Doyle/ Douleur d'Après Doyle
   For Two Weeks I have been in this Palace. Nothing has Happened/ یکی دو هفته میشود که توی این قصرم و هیچ اتفاق نیفتاده
   What You Have Read So Far/ تا اینجا که خوانده‌اید
   Eagle/ عقاب
   Tiger/ ببر
   The Crow's Sonnet/ آواز کلاغ
   Song of the Moon Hanging over the Fields of Damascus/ معلقه‌ی ماه روی دشتهای دمشق

   Wild Grass/ علف دیمی
   My Scent that Doesn't Pass/ بوی من که نمی‌آید

4. Bijan Elahi on Translation

   Translators' Introduction
   "On Translation"/ در باب ترجمه by Bijan Elahi

5. Bibliography of Elahi's Work and Translation

6. Acknowledgements

the operating system digital//document
## High Tide of the Eyes

ISBN # 978-1-946031-55-6
Library of Congress Cataloguing-in-Publication #2019947988
copyright © 2019 by BIJAN ELAHI in translation
by Kayvan Tahmasebian and Rebecca Ruth Gould
edited & designed by ELÆ [Lynne DeSilva-Johnson]
with assistance from Ashkan Eslami Fard
Cover design uses art from Farid Bayan, "My Eyes," from *Under Surveillance* (2012)

is released under a Creative Commons CC-BY-NC-ND (Attribution, Non Commercial, No Derivatives) License: its reproduction is encouraged for those who otherwise could not afford its purchase in the case of academic, personal, and other creative usage from which no profit will accrue.

Complete rules and restrictions are available at:
http://creativecommons.org/licenses/by-nc-nd/3.0/

For additional questions regarding reproduction, quotation, or to request a pdf for review contact operator@theoperatingsystem.org

*Persian text is set in Ordibehesht and Far.Rooznameh. English text is set in Brandon Grotesque, Minion Pro, Arnhem, Franchise, and OCR-A Standard.*

Your donation makes our publications, platform and programs possible!
We <3 You.

http://theoperatingsystem.org/subscribe-join/

the operating system
www.theoperatingsystem.org
operator@theoperatingsystem.org

مد بینایی

# high tide of the eyes

بیژن الهی

## bijan elahi

*translated by*

### rebecca ruth gould

&

### kayvan tahmasebian

کیوان طهماسبیان

www.ingramcontent.com/pod-product-compliance
Lightning Source LLC
Chambersburg PA
CBHW022011120526
44592CB00034B/777